THE COTTON CLUB

Jim Haskins

Robson Books

FIRST PUBLISHED IN GREAT BRITAIN IN 1985 BY ROBSON BOOKS LTD.,
BOLSOVER HOUSE, 5-6 CLIPSTONE STREET, LONDON W1P 7EB. COPY-
RIGHT © 1977 BY JIM HASKINS

British Library Cataloguing in Publication Data

Haskins, Jim
    The Cotton Club
    1. Cotton Club
    I. Title
    785.42'09747'1   ML3508

ISBN 0-86051-315-7
ISBN 0-86051-336-X Pbk

Grateful acknowledgement is made to the following for permission to reprint
previously published material: Abelard-Schuman, a Division of Thomas Y. Crowell
Company, Inc.: Five brief excerpts from pages 42-46 of *Everything and Nothing: The
Dorothy Dandridge Tragedy* by Dorothy Dandridge and Earl Conrad. Copyright ©
1970 by Abelard-Schuman Limited. Crown Publishers, Inc.: Three brief excerpts
from pages 51, 54, and 81 of *The Longest Street* by Louis Sobol. Copyright © 1968 by
Louis Sobol. Doubleday & Company, Inc.: Three brief excerpts from pages 35, 68 and
76 of *Harold Arlen: Happy With the Blues* by Edward Jablonski, Copyright © 1961 by
Edward Jablonski.

Frontispiece: Cab Calloway. (Culver Pictures)
Published by arrangement with the author

Printed in Hungary

For J.M.

Author's Note

This book, *The Cotton Club,* was first published in 1977, when reawakened interest in the heyday of Harlem was evident in the success of the musical *Bubbling Brown Sugar* on Broadway.

Producer Robert Evans had a different vision. He optioned *The Cotton Club* as the basis for a major motion picture for which, six years later, on a sound stage in Astoria, Queens, on East 23rd Street in Manhattan, and up in Harlem itself, director Francis Ford Coppola would recreate a vanished world—Harlem in the 1920s, the Jazz Age, when whites merrily invaded the "capital of black America" to drink Prohibition beer, rub elbows with the mob, and be entertained by the fabled New Negro who represented the exoticism, creativity, and uninhibited naïveté that white folks had lost to the Machine Age.

In those days, the night streets of Harlem dazzled with revelry, there was a speakeasy on every block, and stretch limousines regularly discharged Blue Book socialites come for pre-dawn partying at Harlem's most famous playground. A whites-only nightclub in the heart of Harlem, a club run by gangsters whose clientele included the elite of New York society, the Cotton Club was a bastion of glamorous contradiction and the perfect symbol of its era.

When the era ended—when Prohibition was repealed and the gangsters started fighting over the remaining vices, when the Depression set in and even the most myopic revelers could not ignore the Harlem breadlines—so did the Cotton Club. But its memory lived on. The names of the entertainers who made it famous are famous still, and the yearning for the luxury of carefree exuberance still lurks in the hearts of us all.

The movie *The Cotton Club,* now opened in theaters across the country, tells only part of that fascinating story; for while the makers of *The Cotton Club* strove for historical accuracy wherever possible, their awareness of dramatic necessity and of their intended market caused them to create composite characters and to leave out some parts of the club's history. The book *The Cotton Club* presents the true story, and completes the story in the film.

—Jim Haskins
New York, June 1984

Acknowledgments

I am deeply grateful to the people who helped
me with this book. It is always a pleasure to work
with an editor like Toni Morrison, and I thank her for
the opportunity. I am also indebted to Ruth Ann Stewart
and J. M. Stifle for their research work, to Earl Conrad and
Mrs. Helen Armstead-Johnson for their help, to Mary Ellen
Arrington, who typed the manuscript drafts. A special
thank-you to Kathy, without whom this book
would not have been possible. — J. H.

Contents

Chapter 1

HARLEM COMES OF AGE

A major change in the living patterns of American blacks took place in the years surrounding World War I. Formerly, even in the Northern cities, blacks had lived in homogeneous but widely scattered locations. In New York City some Negro districts such as the Tenderloin and San Juan Hill were clearly identifiable and their names immediately recognized. Yet none was more than a few blocks in area. Prior to World War I, small black residential enclaves could be found throughout the city. Thirty-seventh and Fifty-eighth streets, between Eighth and Ninth avenues, were Negro blocks. All the blocks surrounding them were white. There were even Negro blocks in Harlem, which in the eighteen-eighties and nineties was fast developing into a place of exclusive residence, the first affluent white suburb.

White upper-middle-class New Yorkers viewed Harlem with great expectations, chiefly for two reasons. The first was techno-

Opposite: Bert Williams and George Walker. (Schomburg Collection, NYPL)

logical. Between 1878 and 1881 Manhattan's three elevated railroad lines were extended to 129th Street, and plans for extension farther north were on the books. Previously Harlem's major drawback had been its distance from the city's core; the elevateds would make it accessible. The other factor was immigration. Thousands of Europeans were descending on the city, and in 1880 the population passed the one-million mark. The immigrants settled and established ethnic enclaves, and older white residents fled. As Harlem's transporta-

tion facilities improved, so did its residential prospects, and land speculators quickly moved in to make their fortunes. Town houses and exclusive apartment houses went up as fast as the land on which to put them could be purchased.

Meanwhile, as Harlem was being prepared to welcome upper-class New Yorkers, the city's black population mushroomed. The advance guard of the "Great Migration" began to arrive in the large Northern urban centers about 1890, and in New York the Negro population

Harlem: 133rd Street between Lenox and Fifth avenues. Photo by Grossman, 1939. (Museum of the City of New York)

would nearly triple in the next twenty years. The new arrivals crowded into the small and scattered black sections and pushed their boundaries outward. Early on, it was clear to any thoughtful observer of the urban scene that a large and homogeneous black residential section would eventually develop. But few could have foreseen that the section would be Harlem.

The bottom fell out of the Harlem real estate market in 1904–1905. Too late, speculators realized that too many buildings had been erected too fast, that the price of land and the cost of houses had been inflated way out of proportion to their true value. In their frenzy to recoup their losses, speculators and realtors turned, directly and indirectly, to the Negro. Some opened their buildings to black tenants, who were traditionally charged higher rents than other ethnic groups. Others used the threat of renting to blacks to force white neighbors to purchase vacant buildings at inflated prices. Many white residents of Harlem were willing to pay any price to keep out blacks, and nearly all were against

El Curve at 110th Street, 1898. Drawing by Charles Graham.
(Museum of the City of New York)

Harlem Comes of Age

Harlem ca. 1915. (Brown Bros., Sterling, Pa.)

having Negro neighbors. But the various white groups were never able to muster a united front, and blacks began to move into Harlem in large numbers, many occupying apartment houses that had never been previously rented. Harlem was a "decent neighborhood," and for many of the new black residents it was the first time they had ever been able to live in one.

Black churches moved uptown from the older Negro sections, following their congregations, and by the early nineteen-twenties practically every major black institution had moved from its downtown location to Harlem. While similar develop-

ments had occurred in other large cities like Chicago and Philadelphia, Harlem was unique among Northern urban black enclaves. Not only was it the only black community to form in an exclusive residential section but also it was the largest black community in the United States.

The very name Harlem took on magical connotations to American blacks. Langston Hughes wrote of emerging from the subway at 135th Street and Lenox Avenue and exulting at the sight of so many fellow blacks; he wanted to shake hands with all of them. Harlem became the largest black audience in the country, ripe for Marcus

Garvey and his Back to Africa movements and for A. Philip Randolph and his labor-organizing activities. Harlem, too, represented money, as did New York in general.

The blacks who moved into Harlem prior to the war were monied people, able to afford the high rents charged in the new buildings. Like most upper-middle-class Americans, they formed their own bridge clubs and social clubs, held cocktail parties and exclusive dances, and supported the rapidly growing cultural life of Harlem. Later, working-class blacks were able to move into the area distinguished by spanking-new buildings and broad tree-lined avenues. During the war, jobs were numerous in the munitions and war-materials factories, and black workers were actively recruited by Northern industries. (In this case, for once, European immigrants helped American blacks, although indirectly. When war broke out in Europe, thousands of immigrants returned to fight for their native lands. New immigration virtually ceased, leaving an unprecedented shortage of labor and a new demand for black workers.)

War-inflated wages enabled many blacks to pay the exorbitant Harlem rents and still save, and with their savings they invested in Harlem property. All classes bought, and it was not unusual for a black woman who made her living by taking in laundry to purchase a house. Among the best-known seekers of this ultimate American dream was Mrs. Mary Dean, known as ''Pig Foot Mary'' for the Southern delicacy she vended, pushcart style, in the streets of Harlem; she made a fortune in real estate dealings.

During and after the war, fraternal/social organizations increased rapidly in Harlem, and lodge meetings and lodge halls abounded. In the warm months hardly a Sunday passed when one lodge or another did not celebrate a founding, or honor a

Above: smartly dressed members of the Arrow Tennis Club, c. 1928. (Schomburg Collection, NYPL)
Below: Paul Laurence Dunbar Apartments, at 150th and 151st streets, built by Rockefeller in the 1920s for middle-class Negroes. (Schomburg Collection, NYPL)

Above: Sugar Hill, Edgecombe Avenue, 1938.
(Schomburg Collection, NYPL)
Below: Byron/Harlem Opera House, c. 1906.
(Museum of the City of New York)

deceased member, or simply turn out to represent its standing in the community. Other service enterprises, such as funeral parlors, real estate offices, laundries, were opened by blacks to serve the Harlem community.

Simultaneously the seamy side of Harlem life developed. Legitimate service enterprises were matched by numbers operations, houses of prostitution, dope peddlers. And despite wartime and postwar prosperity, a sizable poor class was growing whose wages could not meet the exorbitant rents, who partitioned off their large apartments and rented rooms and half-rooms to newcomers. By the early twenties, overcrowding was already turning parts of Harlem into slums.

Yet Harlem in the early twenties was chiefly a prosperous black community, its inhabitants proud of their neighborhoods, aware of their strength in numbers. Harlem was not a section that one "went out to"; it was not separated from the rest of the city the way most Negro sections were in other cities. It was neither a slum nor a quarter, but a well-lit, well-paved, well-kept area linked to downtown Manhattan by major avenues and means of public transportation. It was new and growing, and for outsiders it meant opportunity.

Not only laborers came to seek their fortune in Harlem. Those with talent and creativity, and those with pretensions to talent and creativity, were drawn to the place where the widest black audience could be reached, where they could live in a community inhabited almost entirely by fellow blacks. And the more self-confident and articulate blacks came to Harlem, the more attractive it became for still others.

They came—Fritz Pollard, All-American halfback, who sold Negro stock to prosperous black physicians; Paul Robeson, All-American end, preparing to go to law school, unaware that the stage would

intervene; the songwriting team of Creamer and Layton, who had written "After You've Gone" and twelve more songs, and who would later write "Strut, Miss Lizzie"; singers Ethel Waters and Florence Mills, trying to launch their careers; writers like Claude McKay and James Weldon Johnson and Langston Hughes; Preacher Harry Bragg, Harvard Jimmie MacLendon, Bert Williams; a host of other entrepreneurs, artists, writers, actors, singers, all seeking their fortune and each other.

In greater numbers still came the musicians, a large influx of jazz musicians, especially blues players from the South. The dance craze that swept the country between 1914 and 1918 had created a need for violinists and drummers when previously a single pianist had been sufficient. And after the war, small groups including horns began to arrive, attracted by stories that both work and money were abundant in New York.

There was plenty of work for these musicians in Harlem, for as black Manhattanites

Harlem Protest March, East St. Louis Race Riots, 1917. (Schomburg Collection, NYPL)

Opposite: Jack Johnson, heavyweight champion being decorated with forget-me-nots, the chosen tag of the Music Hall Ladies' Guild Orphanage. (Bettmann Archive)

had moved north, so too had the raths-kellers, following the trade. These primarily white-owned establishments, which took their name from the German word meaning cellar beer garden, had been localized in the Forties bordering on Sixth Avenue in the Hell's Kitchen district, site of one of the largest concentrations of black Manhattanites. Following the 1910 victory of black heavyweight boxer Jack Johnson over "Great White Hope" Jim Jeffries, however, outraged whites rioted, smashing, among other establishments in the "Negro Section," the rathskellers. Rather than reopen at their old locations, many rathskeller owners chose to relocate in the fast-growing residential area of Harlem.

The new Harlem establishments were not commonly located in cellars, and the term rathskeller fell into disuse. Only two of these transplanted nightspots were owned by blacks; the rest were owned by Irish: Connors' (operated by John Connors, who, unlike the others, had moved to Harlem from Brooklyn, where he had operated the Royal Café), at 135th Street near Lenox; Edmond's, on Fifth Avenue at 130th Street; LeRoy's, at 135th Street and Fifth Avenue.

They were smoke-misty rooms filled with conversation and laughter, flowing with bad booze. Some were furnished with oddly assorted chairs and white porcelain tables, others with linen-covered tables and velvet-smooth floors. In many, the entertainment consisted of one piano and one female blues singer, her hoarse voice rising vainly over the babble. Larger establishments usually featured a small band or combo, whose size often depended on the volume and economic status of the audi-

ence. The common arrangement between musicians and club management was to place a bowl or cigar box in a central location, and to divide its contents equally among the musicians at the end of the evening. Often the accessibility of the box or bowl caused difficulties. Willie "The Lion" Smith played LeRoy's in those days. He recalls having to install a mirror on top of the piano in order to keep an eye on the cigar box and the singers, musicians and waiters, who were prone to dip into the till for themselves.

The clientele of these nightspots was chiefly black, although in some it was not uncommon to find, over in a corner, a group of whites huddling and grinning and believing they were having a thoroughly wild time. Slumming, it was called. The black patrons paid little attention to them.

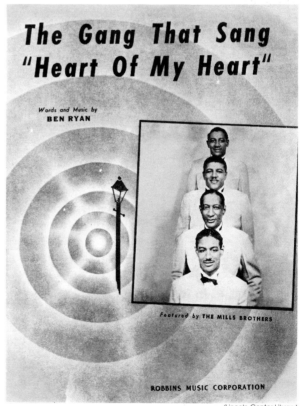

(Lincoln Center Library)

Harlem Comes of Age

11

In other Harlem cabarets, whites were rarely seen except as guests of blacks, and were often unwelcome even on that basis.

The following incident, related by a writer of the day, was typical of the blacks' attitude:

There was a public dance in the old Palace Casino one night. Two white fellows walked in the place and commenced dancing with some of the ladies of color. Immediately there was a young riot. The ladies and gentlemen stormed the manager's office, and threatened all kinds of wild happenings if the white intruders were not ejected. The manager ordered the music stopped, and with a great show of race patriotism, ordered the two men to go downtown and dance with their white women and stop breaking up his business. I have seen this duplicated at the Renaissance [Casino] and other places in a lesser degree.[1]

Most white New Yorkers south of the city's "Mason-Dixon Line," 110th Street, remained relatively unaware of what was going on in Harlem. Certainly most had heard of Marcus Garvey, but he was considered a comical figure by the white downtowners. A. Philip Randolph had made little headway and indeed would not make any for another ten years. The talents of an Ethel Waters or a Noble Sissle or a Eubie Blake were unknown, and white publishers had not as yet taken much interest in black books. Comparatively few whites were interested in Harlem, and fewer still were aware that Harlem was beginning to experience a period of great creativity, born of the coming together of a variety of people and styles. Black writers and poets from across the country met and shared their dreams and their attitudes about being black in America. They talked for hours in small dark cabarets and crowded apartments, reading their latest work to fellow writers, helping each other find housing, food, jobs, encouraging each other. New writing styles and new ways of looking at themselves and the world developed from this interchange.

Among the most notable groups were the young black poets, who seemed to emerge simultaneously about five or six years after the war. James Weldon Johnson, writing in 1930, identified some fifteen poets as writing "verse of distinction" in the early twenties, four fifths of them residing either in New York or Washington, D.C. In 1922 Johnson published The Book of American Negro Poetry, an anthology of poetry that included works by many of these younger writers. Black fiction, too, was suddenly imbued with new life. W. E. B. Du Bois' novel The Quest of the Silver Fleece and James Weldon Johnson's The Autobiography of an Ex-Colored Man were published early in the decade, and in 1923 came Jean Toomer's Cane. Black writers exhibited a new boldness in treating the conditions of Negro life. The following year Walter White wrote of the black existence in a small Southern town in The Fire in the Flint, and Jessie Fauset applied the same techniques of realism in writing about Negro life in a Northern city in There Is Confusion.

Cash prizes for literary work established around 1924 by the National Association for the Advancement of Colored People and the New York Urban League provided further stimuli to the Harlem literary movement. They drew young writers to New York, as did the various radical literary magazines and newspapers, some new, some established but imbued with fresh vigor. The Messenger, Challenge, the Voice, the Crusader, the Emancipator, the Negro World provided an unprecedented forum for the works of young black writers.

Negro theater experienced a different evolution. Of all the arts, it enjoyed the greatest strength and popularity in the war years. Between 1910 and 1917 the first true black theater in New York grew up in Har-

lem—a theater in which black performers played to almost totally black audiences. Supported chiefly by the monied bourgeois class, two major Harlem theaters, the Lafayette and the Lincoln, developed excellent stock companies. Small theater groups abounded. It was an era of great creativity, spurred by isolation, for the years when black theater was at its height in Harlem were also years during which black shows were essentially banned from Broadway. In the early twenties, while the other arts were incubating in Harlem, black theater was being reintroduced downtown and would eventually lead to the birth of the popular Harlem Renaissance.

Meanwhile a period of creativity similar to that in the literary area was occurring in the area of black music, and out of it would come the first New York jazz style. Jazz, as an identifiable style, was relatively new. A product of slave songs containing African elements, black spirituals, urban blues, it represented a synthesis of these styles into new rhythms born of subtle changes in syncopation and timing. More important, it was characterized by improvisation, with rhythmic subtleties that defied

Otis C. Butler/Interior Decorations Shop, c. 1926. (Schomburg Collection, NYPL)

notation. Jazz was not written down, and to the society at large this was pure heresy. It was equally distasteful to most veteran black musicians. Ragtime, which enjoyed its greatest popularity between 1890 and World War I, and which contributed to the development of jazz, had represented a departure from traditional forms. But while it pitted complex African syncopation against a strong basic beat, ragtime was not improvised but carefully worked out, and usually written down.

By the end of World War I a definite jazz style had developed in New Orleans; there were also identifiable Chicago and Kansas City styles. But New York musicians had remained so conservative as to have no real style of their own. Between 1918 and 1921, stimulated by the influx of out-of-town musicians, young trombonists Charlie Irvis and Joe Nanton and trumpeters June Clark and Bubber Miley, among others, had begun to improvise and thus to take the first tentative steps toward a new style. They were criticized by the veteran musicians who resisted the change. In June 1921,

Byron/Mrs. Robinson's Beauty Parlor, c. 1919. (Museum of the City of New York)

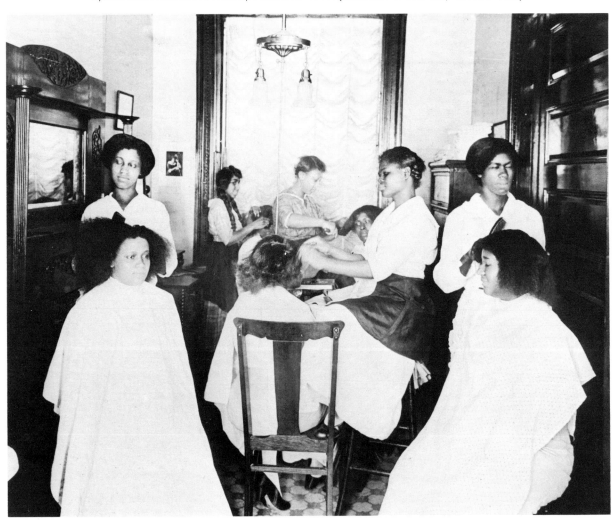

J. Tim Brymn sermonized in a speech before five hundred members of the Clef Club:

"The different bands should follow their orchestrations more closely and not try so much of their 'ad lib' stuff. There is a growing tendency to make different breaks, discords and other things which make a lot of noise and jumble up the melody until it is impossible to recognize it. White musicians have excelled colored players because they are willing to supply novelty music and let it be done by the publisher's arranger, who knows how to do it. If you find it necessary to improve on an orchestration have it done on paper so that the improved way of playing will be uniform and always the same."[2]

Casper Holstein entertaining at ladies' club, c. 1923. (Schomburg Collection, NYPL)

While they may have been constrained to follow on-paper orchestrations when playing with the veterans and before formal audiences, the young musicians found encouragement for their tuneful ad-libbing on the streets of Harlem. Jazz was everywhere—on the corners, in the alleys, in sparerib joints. Vagabond musicians abounded, sought each other out, helped each other, learned from one another. It was a time of tremendous inventiveness, of spur-of-the-moment creativity. Faint but exciting sounds wafted across 110th Street. The ears of the uninitiated perked up and curious eyes looked northward.

White interest, and more important, white money, would help bring Harlem downtown and white downtowners uptown, would spur greater creativity and would give birth to the Harlem Renaissance, as future generations would know it. While many would prefer to believe that this renaissance would have occurred in spite of whites, evidence suggests that without them it would not have assumed the major proportions it eventually reached.

The event most frequently cited as the beginning of the commercial Harlem Renaissance is the revue Shuffle Along,

which opened at the 63rd Street Music Hall on May 22, 1921. It was not the first black show to penetrate to the heart of Broadway; certainly black-influenced minstrel shows had played the Great White Way for years, and black theater had been an important aspect of the American entertainment industry for years before that. Until 1891 the shows presented by black entertainers had been of the strict minstrel variety, but in that year an ambitious Negro undertaking, The Creole Show, which glorified black women, opened in Chicago. It contained many elements of the traditional minstrel shows, but it also represented the beginning of an evolution in black shows that would lead directly to the musical comedies of Cole and Johnson and Williams and Walker. While it never actually made Broadway, it came very close by playing the old Standard Theatre in Greeley Square, the edge of the "Broadway zone." The Creole Show was widely imitated in the next few years, but the minstrel format (a potpourri of acts with a male interlocutor prominent) was retained. A Trip to Coontown, which opened in 1898, was the first black show to break completely with this tradition, the first to be written with

continuity and to have a cast of characters working out a story from beginning to end.

In ensuing years, composers began to write musical scores for such productions, and in 1902 the first completely black show, In Dahomey, opened in the very center of the theater district, the New York Theatre in Times Square. Produced by the well-known comedy team of Williams and Walker, with a score by Will Marion Cook and lyrics by Paul Laurence Dunbar, the show later went to London and played a royal command performance at Buckingham Palace on June 23, 1903. It was followed, in 1906, by In Abyssinia, also starring Williams and Walker, and by Bandana Land in 1907. Both were highly successful shows, and it seemed that Broadway was now open country for Williams and Walker, that black shows were there to stay.

But during the run of Bandana Land, George Walker fell ill, never to return to the stage again. Bert Williams appeared alone in A Lode of Kole in 1909, but the magic of the Williams/Walker duo was gone, and it was the last black show in which he ever appeared. The following year he joined the Ziegfeld Follies. That same year the almost simultaneous deaths of three outstanding creators and performers—Ernest Hogan, Bob Cole and George Walker—signaled the end of this great era of black theater. Except for Bert Williams, whose famous solo acts enlivened the Ziegfeld Follies for some years afterward, black talent was abandoned by Broadway.

Black theater remained alive in New York, but in Harlem, not downtown. It was welcomed and supported by the Harlem community and enjoyed a tremendous period of creativity between 1910 and 1917, marked especially by the productions at the Lincoln and Lafayette theaters. While Shuffle Along is generally considered the catalyst for downtown interest in Harlem, the first show actually to bring Broad-

Opposite: The vivacious Josephine Baker. (Culver Pictures)

way up to Harlem opened at the Lafayette Theatre in 1913. Darktown Follies was written and staged by Leubrie Hul, a former member of the Williams and Walker company. It was the subject of headlines and cartoons in the New York papers, and going to Harlem to see it became fashionable. Florenz Ziegfeld saw the show and bought the rights to produce the finale to the first act and several numbers in his own Follies. Had societal conditions been different, the Harlem vogue might well have started then. But World War I broke out, and national as well as New York attention turned to other matters. During the war years some old talent and some new dreamed of returning the black show to Broadway.

That return began one summer evening in Philadelphia in 1920. The NAACP was giving a benefit, and among the acts scheduled to perform were the musical vaudeville duo of Noble Sissle and Eubie Blake and the comedy vaudeville team of Flournoy E. Miller and Aubrey Lyles. After the show both sets of performers met and decided to join forces to try to put the Negro back on Broadway. Less than a year later they did so, with a splash.

Shuffle Along was a swift, bright, rollicking show, crammed with talent. Hall Johnson, later a famous choir director, and composer William Grant Still were in the orchestra. Sissle and Blake, in addition to having written the music, played and acted in the show. Miller and Lyles outdid themselves in their comedy routines. Florence Mills's career skyrocketed after her performance in the second act. Josephine Baker was in the chorus.

Shuffle Along was cast in the best Wiliams and Walker tradition, but its music was

completely nontraditional. In fact, the success of Shuffle Along was due chiefly to its music and its choreography, for it legitimized ragtime music and jazz dancing. Many of its tunes, among them "I'm Just Wild about Harry," "Love Will Find a Way" and "In Honeysuckle Time," became world-famous. In the earlier shows, ragtime had been hidden under the heavy overlay of operetta. By the time the show opened in New York, Blake had already won fame as a composer, and ragtime was present in pure form in Shuffle Along, providing white society the first real opportunity to hear, see and enjoy this first distinctly American music. Certainly there was some awareness of the blues, for example, but it, like the cabarets, was considered lower-class and associated too closely with blacks. As one writer put it:

One is elevated by the drama, music and scenery of the opera. He brings away something worth while. In the cabaret, however (which is usually plunged deep beneath the ground, free from ventilation, where one's clothes become thoroughly saturated with tobacco smoke and where no complaints of the ordinary passerby can be made against this generally recognized impossible music), he gets jaded, exhausted by the monotony and noise, finally returning to his home physically, mentally and financially depleted . . . it takes a much higher degree of education and training to produce operas than it does to write scrolls of the "blues." Also, a race that hums operas will stay ahead of a race that simply hums the "blues."[3]

Jazz struck a responsive chord in white society, and soon became the rage. Thousands flocked to the 63rd Street Music Hall to listen to the ragtime music and to watch and try to learn the jazz dancing. Responding to this new interest, "colored dance" studios opened up, many on Broadway, to teach black dance styles like the "snake-hips" to eager whites. Among the best-

known and popular teachers was Billy Pearce. In his autobiography, critic Leonard Sillman recalled; "One day when I came to Billy's for a lesson I looked into one of the studios and got an interesting view of a matronly female standing beside a victrola . . . She was getting ready to go into 'Scarlet Sister Mary.' To get the Negro rhythm, the Negro feel, Ethel Barrymore was studying Snake Hips at Billy Pearce's."[4]

Before long, this interest in the music and dancing of Shuffle Along shifted to an interest in Harlem. After all, downtown whites surmised, if such exciting things were happening in a black show on Broadway, it followed that even more exciting things were happening up in Harlem. What, indeed, was going on up there?

Carl Van Vechten was one who told them. A music critic who had also turned to fiction in 1920, Van Vechten had been impressed with black music for years, far in advance of most other whites. He now began to write magazine articles about the creative movement in Harlem, at the same time visiting Harlem and getting to know the writers and singers and musicians. They welcomed his sincere interest. His new acquaintances became the subjects of more magazine articles. White New Yorkers read these articles avidly, but they were not long content merely to read about what was going on. Soon they wanted to see for themselves.

A decade before, the white public would not have risen to the opportunity of enjoying and appreciating jazz. But in the post-war period, a fast and feverish era in the industrial development of the country was at hand. The war had radically changed national attitudes and the national rhythm. While for many it had signified a coming of age, in the view of others the significance was much less positive. The occurrence of a world war had resulted also in a loss of innocence. Some would call it a loss of

ignorance, and applaud. But it was an unsettling experience to recognize the economic and political machinations that had led to U.S. involvement in the European war. The nation had lost its open faith in itself and in mankind. The war had caused many Americans to view the world differently, less optimistically, to take pride in a worldly cynicism but at the same time to mourn the passing of more naïve days.

For most Americans the vague sense of unrest never reached conscious expression. Had the end of the war brought a sudden economic depression, the national mood might have been different. But wartime prosperity continued into the postwar era, and surface contentment reigned. Outright cynicism was expressed primarily by urban intellectuals and the urban wealthy. The intellectuals looked with distaste at the war-stimulated mass industrialization, bemoaned, as Carl Van Vechten put it, the "Machine Age," that "profound national impulse [that] drives the hundred millions steadily toward uniformity." They attacked the middle class and its values as puritanical and life-denying. Pseudointel-

Renaissance Ballroom, 1927. (Collection of Duncan Schiedt)

lectuals responded eagerly to the call, and cynicism became fashionable.

Urban "society" took up the fad. Wealthy sons and daughters revolted against the boredom of proper lives. The daughters led the way. A new age of freedom for girls was beginning. Women's rights, women's suffrage—the war had nurtured such ideas. Their men gone to war, the women of America had been forced in greater numbers than ever before to be independent and self-reliant. To be sure, it was the women of the lower economic classes who had worked in the war products factories and headed families, but it

was on the backs of such women that the young socialites rode to adventure.

Harlem, and the Negro, seemed to embody the primitive and thrilling qualities sought by both intellectuals and socialites. To the intelligentsia, innocence was still alive in America in the Negro. In the Negro was all the sensuousness and life rhythm that white America had lost. To the socialites, Harlem represented a blend of danger and excitement. The exotic jungle rhythms gave intimations of sensuality beyond the wildest fantasies of the sons and daughters of proper New York society. Not that these fantasies were particularly inspired. Sex in

Exterior view of the Cotton Club, 1937 (UPI)

the twenties was quite tame. As Anita Loos put it: "How could any epoch boast of passion with its hit song bearing the title, 'When You Wore a Tulip, a Bright Yellow Tulip, and I Wore a Big Red Rose'?" Four-letter words were barred from popular books; pornography was accessible only to those with connections. Certainly "race records" with "blue" songs were available, but even these were much more implicit than explicit in their sexuality. A passionate tango rendition or a snapped garter in a dark corner were highly titillating experiences. Harlem was an adventure; Harlem was the unknown; and Harlem became a fad.

The Negro was in vogue, and in Harlem the speakeasy took on a new dimension. White downtowners invaded Harlem to observe the blacks at play, "flooding the little cabarets and bars where formerly only colored people laughed and sang, and where now the strangers were given the best ringside tables to sit and stare at the Negro customers—like amusing animals in a zoo."[5]

"White people," the black newspaper New York Age, commented, "are taking a morbid interest in the nightlife of [Harlem]." Some of the owners of the Harlem clubs, delighted at the flood of white patronage, encouraged their employees to give the white folks a good show. Waiters danced the jig or the Charleston as they waited tables. At the Savoy Ballroom, the dancers were inspired to unheard-of acrobatic feats for the entertainment of the white observers. More often, however, the black patrons of the clubs merely acted as they always had, which was neither African nor exotic, and in time, tired of being stared at, they ceased to patronize the clubs.

Most Harlemites were suspicious of white people's interest in them. They were accustomed to being shunned by whites, not

Program. (Lincoln Center Library)

sought by them. The memory of white reaction to Jack Johnson's victory was vivid. White people just didn't do such an about-face; they had simply found a new way to exploit blacks.

A kinship exists between this stereotype [of the New Negro] and that of the contented slave; one is merely a "jazzed-up" version of the other, with cabarets supplanting cabins, and Harlemized "blues," instead of the spirituals and slave reels.[6]

In the minds of New York's white leisure class, the change in the Negro's image took place in a remarkably short time. Rudolph Fisher, known at the time as one of the wittiest blacks in Harlem, was a writer as well as a physician. He had been away at medical school during the rise and

establishment of the Harlem vogue. Returning to New York, he immediately went to his favorite basement spot, where he had once enjoyed the company of other young blacks, and ignored the occasional party of white slummers in the corner. "I remembered one place especially where my own crowd used to hold forth; and, hoping to find some old-timers there still, I sought it out one midnight. 'What a lot of "fays"!' I thought as I noticed the number of white guests. Presently I grew puzzled and began to stare, then I gasped—and gasped. I found myself wondering if this was the right place—if, indeed, this was Harlem at all. I suddenly became aware that, except for the waiters and members of the orchestra, I was the only Negro in the place."[7]

Fisher was in for another surprise. In the heart of Harlem, there were now white establishments!

A combination of elements gave rise to the Harlem Renaissance and to white interest in the so-called New Negro. So, too, a combination of many of the same elements created the climate out of which these "white clubs" arose, but here there

was an additional, and major factor—Prohibition. It would, in a very fundamental way, divide the Harlem Renaissance into two parts—that of the black writers and intellectuals and that of the black musicians and performers. The former made their mark, or didn't, regardless of the Volstead Act of 1919. The latter owed much to Prohibition, for had it not been for this attempt at legally enforced abstention, organized crime would not have moved into Harlem—at least not as early or with such vigor.

Most of the Irish cabaret owners moved out, and mostly Italians came in, although Dutch, German, Jewish and French mobsters were well represented, and some of the Irish simply made alterations in their already established businesses.

The mob bosses took people's desire for bootleg liquor, coupled it with the interest of high-living white downtowners in Harlem, and parlayed the combination into the most profitable underworld business ever, until dope came along. And it was not long before the gangsters discovered they were an added attraction themselves. The "jet set" of the twenties felt a kinship with the bootleggers in flouting the law. White gangsters acquired a romantic image

I bring you my songs
To sing on the Georgia roads
—Langston Hughes

tinged with danger, and many played the role conscientiously, with their snap-brim Capone hats pulled low over their eyes, shoulders hunched, coat collars turned up and hands buried deep in their overcoat pockets. Bugsie Siegel became the most fascinating man around New York, and the American Princess Dorothy di Frasso the envy of many Park Avenue debutantes for attracting him.

Within a few years after the Prohibition law was enacted, a number of prosperous clubs catering to white sightseers had opened in Harlem. Many of them were located on 133rd Street between Lenox and Seventh avenues in a neighborhood known as "Beale Street," a name made famous by W. C. Handy. But wherever their location, their basic formulae were the same: (1) cater primarily to whites and give them everything they want—an opportunity to observe exotic entertainment, a chance to participate without crossing, to any appreciable degree, the color line, a chance to be in but not of Harlem, (2) and more important, sell a lot of bootleg liquor.

Some actively barred blacks; others were willing to serve whoever could pay. But in nearly all clubs there was a substantial white presence, a presence not open to question or criticism. As the writer who described the Palace Casino incident put it:

... who would think of ordering white people out of a colored dance in Harlem today, unless it was a private or a club function? The white people come in larger numbers today and have acquired a financial interest in Harlem's social life, especially the night life. The same manager would perhaps throw a Negro out today if he protested, on the grounds of breaking up his business. The same ladies who squawked so loudly that night about the presence of white men would be boasting today that New York is so cosmopolitan, or, perhaps, Bohemian.[8]

Exterior view of the Cotton Club, 1937
(Collection of Duncan Schiedt)

These clubs existed side by side with Harlem characters like the Messiah, who walked the streets barefoot, summer and winter, urging the people he passed to "Repent!," and with the New York City police, who acted more as a security force for the clubs than as protectors of the people in the neighborhood. The clubs existed in spite of the Committee of Fourteen, a self-appointed group of Prohibition-minded citizens who branded the Harlem nightclub district a menace, and in spite of the moralizers against sex and racial mixing who seemed, like the Prohibitionists, to spend an inordinate amount of time "studying" the area in order to identify its sins.

Rollin Kirby caricatured the figure of Prohibition as suspiciously red-nosed, suspiciously tipsy and carrying a bottle in his hip
pocket. The writer Hendrik de Leeuw quite
effectively caricatured himself and other
anti-sin crusaders when he wrote about
Harlem in his Sinful Cities of the Western
World:

I beheld brown-skin vamps and other gay colored silhouettes, romp from lantern post to post.
I saw white women trot along, prancing and
strutting with negroes . . . swarms of people with
banjoes and ukes strumming, gurgling sensual
music, while from side streets one could almost
hear the heavy snoring of dusky inhabitants,
sleeping the sleep of the jungle man . . .
I came to the Night Club . . . This place is
said to be the most exclusive in the Black and
Tan. Negroes—superbly dressed American
women, waiters carrying heavily laden trays with
booze for Americans that know not how to
drink—whites on top of blacks, red and yellow
lights flashing over moving bodies—a colored
wench, gorgeously attired, with a face like a
mongrel and a beetle brow—all gliding and
prancing and swinging and prowling, impeded
me as I fought my way to the door—where
many feet deep stood another mob, aching
to get in.[9]

Each club had its own particular flavor.
Many changed hands several times in the
initial scramble to exploit the New Negro/
bootleg liquor business. Some became
famous only to New Yorkers, others to most
Americans. Some survived for many years,
others for only a few. There was Broadway
Jones's Supper Club, which was opened by

the popular tenor vocalist at 65 West 129th Street about 1920. In 1919, following the opening of a new Sissle-Blake revue entitled <u>Bamville</u>, the club's name was changed to the Bamville Club. The club gave a ''welcome home'' banquet for Florence Mills upon her return from Europe in 1927. She died one week later.

There was Barron's (Wilkins) Exclusive Club. Barron D. Wilkins had already run an established enterprise, the Little Savoy, in the midtown Tenderloin district (West 35th Street) before moving up to Harlem to open a club bearing his name around 1915. Obviously possessing an ear for musi-

cal talent, Wilkins employed, in those early Harlem years, such performers as Willie ''The Lion'' Smith, Ada ''Brick Top'' Smith, and Elmer Snowden's Washingtonians, of which Duke Ellington was a member and would later be leader.

There was the Clam House, at 131 West 133rd Street, a favorite early-morning eating spot, where Gladys Bentley dressed in male attire and entertained the guests with naughty songs.

There was Connie's Inn, on the corner of 131st Street and Seventh Avenue. Originally it was opened as the Shuffle Inn in November 1921 by Jack Goldberg, who

Duke Ellington's Washingtonians. (Collection of Duncan Schiedt)

attempted to capitalize on the success of Shuffle Along on Broadway. At the time, George and Connie Immerman were in the delicatessen business, employing ''Fats'' Waller as a delivery boy. When the Immermans decided to go into the Harlem nightclub business, they selected the Shuffle Inn for, among other reasons, its excellent location. In front of its Seventh Avenue façade was Harlem's famous Tree of Hope.

Connie's Inn became one of the three most popular nightspots in Harlem. Its peak period came in 1929 when Louis Armstrong came in from Chicago to star in the show Hot Chocolates. ''Fats'' Waller and Andy Razaf wrote the score for the show, which played simultaneously at the Hudson Theatre on West Forty-Sixth Street. ''Ain't Misbehavin''' and ''Can't We Get Together?'' were two of the songs that came out of that show.

There was Ed Small's Paradise, opened around 1925 by a former elevator operator and a descendant of the black Civil War hero Captain Robert Smalls. With Connie's Inn, it became another of the three most successful night clubs in Harlem during Prohibition. There was the Nest Club, and Pod's and Jerry's, the Silver Dollar Café, and the Breakfast Club, Connor's and the Hollywood Cabaret . . .

. . . And there was the Cotton Club, the first in fame of Harlem's ''Big Three'' night clubs of the era. Some would add, ''First in notoriety,'' for its ''whites only'' admittance

Above: Small's Paradise exterior, 1928.
(Collection of Duncan Schiedt)
Below: Interior of Nest Club. (Schomburg Collection, NYPL)

policy, but others would add, ''First and foremost in bringing Broadway to Harlem . . . and Harlem to Broadway.'' Whatever the reasons, there are few Americans over age twenty who have not heard of the Cotton Club. This is why.

Chapter 2

 THE COTTON CLUB

About 1918 a building was constructed for amusement purposes on the northeast corner of 142nd Street and Lenox Avenue. Built to compete with the very successful Renaissance Casino on West 133rd Street, the Douglas Casino was, like the Renaissance, a two-story building and intended as a dual operation. On the street floor was the Douglas Theatre, which featured films and occasional vaudeville acts such as magicians and strong men. One flight up was a huge room, originally intended to be a dance hall. Plans to book some of the big dances, banquets and concerts away from the Renaissance were unsuccessful, and the dance hall remained essentially unused until around 1920. The former heavyweight champion Jack Johnson, who also happened to be an amateur cellist and bull fiddler, and who was a connoisseur of Harlem night life, rented it and turned it into an intimate supper club, the Club Deluxe.

Opposite: Earl ``Snakehips'' Tucker and Bessie Dudley. (Lincoln Center Library)

Even reborn as a supper club, however, the place failed to attract attention, until Owney Madden's gang came around looking for a suitable spot for the entertainment of white downtowners and to serve as the principal East Coast outlet for "Madden's No. 1" beer. The Club Deluxe seated 400–500 people, and it was just the place for which the syndicate was looking. Madden's people made a deal with Johnson under which the group would operate the place but Johnson would be kept on in a semimanagerial position. The ex-fighter eagerly accepted.

Owen "Owney" Madden was not personally involved in the transaction. He was in Sing Sing at the time, having been convicted in 1914 of manslaughter in the killing of one Patsy Doyle in an Eighth Avenue saloon.

Owney Madden had been one of the most notorious of the pre-Prohibition gang leaders. Born in England, he had come to the United States at the age of eleven and had acquired the nickname Owney the Killer when only seventeen years old. He was eighteen when he assumed command of one of the factions of the Gopher Gang, the largest gang in Hell's Kitchen. A slim, dapper young man, he did not have much

"Evolution of the Speakeasy." Lithograph by Joseph Webster Golinkin. (Museum of the City of New York)

interest in the gambling and prostitution operations favored by some of his colleagues. His principal businesses were sneak thievery, stickups, loft burglaries, "protection" contracts with merchants and saloon keepers, and collections from corrupt politicians. He boasted that he had never worked a day in his life and never would.

Madden did not look like a hood; he had the gentlest smile in New York's underworld. But he possessed great cunning and was capable of extreme cruelty. Brash and ambitious, he made no secret of his desire to be king of all the gangs, and he was willing to kill anyone who stood in his way. By the time he was convicted of the Doyle killing, the police had attributed four other murders to him personally and several more to his henchmen.

Owney Madden had many enemies, and there were several attempts on his life after he took over the Gopher faction. None came near to succeeding until the night of November 6, 1912, when Madden went to the Arbor Dance Hall and became interested in a pretty young woman. By the time he noticed the eleven thugs, they had surrounded him and started firing. Surgeons dug six bullets from his body, and it

"Evolution of the Speakeasy." Lithograph by Joseph Webster Golinkin. (Museum of the City of New York)

took him months to recuperate. The word went out to Madden's men, and in less than a week after the shooting, three of the eleven men had been murdered.

With Madden in the hospital, other gangsters sought to take over his territory. Patsy Doyle began spreading the rumor that Madden was permanently crippled. Apparently this rumor disturbed Madden more than others' attempts to displace him, for as soon as he was released from the hospital he set out after Patsy Doyle.

The murder was Madden's undoing. Two or three days after the Doyle killing, Madden was arrested. When he was convicted and sentenced to Sing Sing for ten to twenty years he was just twenty-three years

Owney Madden. (Museum of the City of New York)

old. His conviction and imprisonment had a profound effect on him. Though he would continue to exercise considerable power in the underworld he did so less conspicuously, avoiding as much as possible further trouble with the police and with his underworld enemies.

Despite his confinement, Madden maintained tight control over his syndicate and closely watched trends in the outside society that could be exploited for profit. When the Prohibition law was passed, Madden realized, along with other gang leaders, that to go into the Harlem cabaret field was good business. It was not necessary for him to be present for the actual arrangements; in fact, he preferred otherwise. He shunned publicity, and even after his parole, was seldom seen at the Cotton Club.

Like other syndicate-owned clubs, the new club was run by a "front man." Walter Brooks, who had brought Shuffle Along to the legitimate theater, served in this capacity, assisted at times by Jack Johnson. Madden was listed as a minor officer of the corporation, and the president was a little-known pickpocket named Sam Sellis. But the syndicate realized that there were economic advantages to a certain amount of visibility. George "Big Frenchy" DeMange, one of Madden's closest aides, was made secretary of the corporation formed to operate the club. One of the duties of this rotund, card-playing Frenchman was to spend time at the club, giving the patrons the added kick of rubbing elbows with mobsters.

The Madden people moved in. The first order of business was to change the club's name. The exact derivation of the name Cotton Club is not known, but it is likely that the club's intended "whites only" policy, together with intimations of the South, were behind the choice.

The next concern was to stretch the seat-

Begowned chorus line. (Author's collection)

ing capacity of the room to the limit. In the classic cabaret manner, it was arranged in a horseshoe shape, with the audience seated on two levels. Some of the tables surrounded the dance floor in front of the tiny proscenium stage, some were on a raised area in the back. The walls were lined with booths, and as many tiny tables as could fit were crammed in on both levels. Seating capacity was thus raised to about 700.

The club was refurbished to cater to the white downtowners' taste for the primitive. It was a "jungle décor," with numerous artificial palm trees. Draperies, tablecloths, fixtures were elegant. The idea, like Johnson's, was to create a plush late-night supper club, and to charge prices befitting such luxury.

The menu was designed to appeal to a variety of tastes. Besides the basic steak

and lobster fare, it would offer Chinese and Mexican dishes, as well as a liberal sampling of "Harlem" cuisine, such as fried chicken and barbecued spareribs.

To ensure the loyalty of their workers, the Madden people turned to Chicago for their nonentertainment staff. Busboys, waiters, cooks, the various workers for the syndicate, the hangers-on—all were imported from Chicago. Most of the entertainers came from there, too. Not until 1927 did the Cotton Club band become a non-Chicago group.

There were other restrictions that applied to the entertainers. The chorus girls had to be uniformly "high-yaller," at least 5'6", dancers, and able to carry a tune. And they could not be over twenty-one.

Rounding out the entertainment would be the male dancers, individual acts, brother acts. Skin color was not important

The Cotton Club

in the choice of male dancers. Their dancing ability—high-stepping, gyrating, snake-dancing—was.

It was decided that the Cotton Club floor show should be a multileveled, fast-paced revue, a new one twice a year, staged in a lavish Ziegfeld manner. Lew Leslie, who later gained fame through his Blackbird revues on Broadway, was hired as producer. Boston songwriter Jimmy McHugh, who had acquired a certain amount of fame during World War I with his "Inky Dinky Parlez-Vous," would do the songs, and Andy Preer's orchestra, the Mis-sourians, was brought from Chicago and renamed Andy Preer's Cotton Club Syncopators. Other creators and performers were hired according to a single formula: all those who were involved in production, staging, choreography, set and costume design were talented whites, and all those who performed were talented blacks.

In January 1923, Owney Madden was paroled from Sing Sing, released on good behavior after serving approximately eight years of his ten-to-twenty-year sentence. He left the preparations for the Cotton Club's opening to his lieutenants and associates

Center stage at the Cotton Club, 1934. (UPI)

and concentrated on his beer business, although it is likely that more than beer passed through his downtown factory. A few months after his release from prison, he and five other men were arrested near White Plains, a suburb of New York City, for riding in a truck containing $25,000 worth of stolen liquor. At his arraignment he managed to get the charges dismissed when he told the court he had simply hitched a ride on the truck and did not know what kind of cargo it was carrying.

In the fall of the same year the Cotton Club staged its grand opening. The show was essentially an uptown version of the lavish Negro stage revues that were selling out theaters down on Broadway. The Cotton Club customers had seen these revues and had come uptown to get a closer look. The Cotton Club orchestra thus had to be a show orchestra, playing to an audience that often had just left one of the top revues and wanted to hear music in the same slick commercial style. The Cotton Club girls were beautiful, glamorous, dressed in revealing costumes. The songs were memorable. In those early years, McHugh would introduce such popular

With the chorus girls and boys at the Cotton Club, 1934. (UPI)

The Cotton Club

numbers as "I Can't Believe that You're in Love with Me," "When My Sugar Walks Down the Street" and "Freeze and Melt."

The customers were impressed with the show. More than that, they were impressed with the ambience, the mood of the Cotton Club. Impeccable behavior was expected—demanded—of the guests, particularly while the show was going on. A loud-talking customer would be touched on the shoulder by a waiter. If he persisted in his talking, the captain would politely ask him to keep his voice down. If this attempt was unsuccessful, the headwaiter would remind the customer that he had been warned; and if even this reminder proved futile, the loud talker was thrown out. This policy continued throughout the Cotton Club's Harlem days and was one reason why the club had less trouble than most other Harlem night clubs.

The staff—waiters, busboys—behaved with equal decorum. The waiters at some of the other clubs did the Charleston while balancing their trays; the waiters at the Cotton Club considered such public display in extremely bad taste. But their actions were of more than casual interest to the customers, for their motions were marvels of studied elegance. Everything, from menus to drinks to meals, was served with a flourish. When conspicuous spenders wished to heighten their visibility, the Cotton Club waiters obligingly caused the champagne bottle corks to pop louder and fly higher than usual.

As was the custom in most "speaks," the patrons who did not wish to drink beer brought their own liquor, although those who came unprepared could make a separate deal with the waiter or doorman. A bottle of fairly good champagne could be had for $30 and a fifth of Scotch might cost $18. Beer was less expensive but still costly enough, as were the club's other prices, to keep out undesirable customers.

Among those considered undesirables were blacks, even in, or perhaps particularly in, mixed parties. Carl Van Vechten reported: "There were brutes at the door to enforce the Cotton Club's policy which was opposed to mixed parties." Only the light-

In New York the pungent brew of Mayor Jimmy Walker's administration was being distilled, and Jimmy was seeing to it that every con man worthy of the name had a brimming glassful. Jimmy's was not the undercover graft of the sixties . . . Jimmy was right out there in the open, a comforting assurance to the lowliest panhandler that eminence need not prevent a man from being human.

—Anita Loos, A Girl Like I

Jimmy Durante at the Cotton Club in 1936 with Mayor and Mrs. Zimmerman of Buffalo. (Acme)

est-complexioned Negroes gained entrance, and even they were carefully screened. The club's management was aware that most white downtowners wanted to <u>observe</u> Harlem blacks, not mix with them; or, as Jimmy Durante put it, "it isn't necessary to mix with colored people if you don't feel like it. You have your own party and keep to yourself. But it's worth seeing. How they step!"[1]

The Cotton Club eliminated the need for conflict or guilt—all the performers were black, all the observers were white. Durante suggested another reason for the club's "whites only" policy: "Racial lines are drawn there to prevent possible trouble. Nobody wants razors, blackjacks, or fists flying—and the chances of a war are less if there's no mixing . . ."[2]

Another factor responsible for the club's popularity was that it was among the few clubs that offered entertainment so late at night that the show-business crowd could catch a show there after their own work was done. Their presence, in turn, attracted non-show-business patrons.

It was not long before the Cotton Club became known as the "Aristocrat of Harlem," as Lady Mountbatten dubbed it.

Other clubs opened, all based on the successful Cotton Club idea, some with variations on the theme. Small's Paradise, at 229½ Seventh Avenue, staged a gala opening in the fall of 1925. The large cellar was packed with 1,500 people that evening. Small's also catered to the tastes of the white downtowners. It stayed open later than the Cotton Club and most other

clubs, and its specialty was early-morning breakfast for all-night revelers. The waiters at Small's, copying those of some other clubs, did the Charleston while balancing full trays of bad whiskey. Unlike the Cotton Club, Small's admitted black patrons, although its prices successfully shielded the white downtowners from the ''colored rabble.''

Small's flourished. Many of the others that opened around the same time did not. Most did not last more than two or three weeks; they lacked ''class.'' One was much like the next. The ingredients: bootleg liquor and a good show for the white folks. But as one folded, two more took its place. Harlem was a honeycomb of speakeasies and drinking dives, and these, along with the seven major night clubs and eighteen dance halls for mixed patronage, led the Committee of Fourteen to brand the district a menace.

This was hardly news to the police. They were quite aware of the illicit activities in Harlem, and elsewhere in the city. Their problem was that the small joints were such fly-by-night operations, so ''portable,'' that by the time the cops got inside, the evidence had vanished. As for the big clubs, generally their ''management'' had an understanding with the police and detectives. The clubs ran comparatively clean and peaceful operations, paid regular bribes, and in return the cops let them go about their business. The same arrangement did not hold with the Feds, who were less vulnerable to appeals to personal greed than local law-enforcement officials. The Feds had just as much trouble as the local cops catching the small cabaret owners with incriminating bootleg liquor. But they had considerably greater success with the larger clubs. In June 1925 Federal Court Judge Francis A. Winslow placed a padlock on the Cotton Club's door and on those of eight other clubs, pending resolu-

Above: ''The King is Dead—Long Live the Queen.''
Drawing by Rollin Kirby.
(Museum of the City of New York)
Below: ''United We Stand.'' Drawing by Rollin Kirby.
(Museum of the City of New York)

tion of charges that the clubs had violated Prohibition laws.

Both Madden, as secretary, and Sellis, as president, were named in the indictment, which charged forty-four violations of the Volstead Act. The criminal records of both men were offered by Assistant U.S. Attorney Bellinger as evidence against them. In pleading their case, Madden and Sellis assured Judge Winslow that they had tried to ''make good'' since their last prison sentences. In the end they and the club got off rather lightly, for neither man was sent back to prison; however, a substantial fine was levied against the club, and the loss of revenue resulting from the club's three-month closing constituted a substantial penalty in itself.

When the Cotton Club reopened, several changes had been made, changes that proved to be fortunate for it. Walter Brooks had been replaced as front man by Harry Block, and Herman Stark, who was hired essentially as stage manager, finally found his true calling at the Cotton Club. A former machine gunner, Stark looked like a typical stage manager—gruff, stout, cigar-chewing—but more important, he had the mind and the thinking of a stage manager. Under his direction the Cotton Club reached its apogee. It was Stark who persuaded the club's management to hire Dan Healy to replace Lew Leslie as ''conceiver and producer'' of the Cotton Club shows, and it was under Healy's direction that the shows took on their now famous form.

Healy was young, but already he was a show-business veteran, He was best known for his portrayal on the night of July 16, 1919, when Prohibition went into effect, of the now famous Rollin Kirby caricature that

The creation of Harlem as a place of exotic culture was as much a service to white need as it was to black. So essential has been the Negro personality to the white American psyche that black theatrical masks had become, by the twentieth century, a standard way for whites to explore dimensions of themselves that seemed impossible through their own personae . . . Thus the strands of identity for Afro-Americans in the 1920's were confounded in a tradition of white/black self-concept that could not be unraveled by simple proclamations of the birth of the New Negro.

—Nathan Huggins, Harlem Renaissance

was to represent the figure of Prohibition. On the stage of the Majestic Theatre, Healy, reeling across the stage, a bottle sticking out of his hip pocket, symbolized to perfection "the gaunt, cruel-lipped chap with the funereal get-up, the high hat and the suspiciously boozy nose." Little did he know at the time that some years later he would be hired by an establishment that thumbed its nose at the Prohibition law almost as effectively.

Healy had appeared in legitimate musicals, among others the Rogers and Hart show Betsy, and Kalmar and Ruby's Good Boy. He could dance, sing and do ad-lib comedy, and he was among the most energetic performers around. Still, he was not hired by the Cotton Club for these talents alone, for he also had considerable production experience, some in association with the Madden syndicate. After stag-

ing shows for the Chateau Madrid, for "Legs" Diamond's Frolics, and for shows in Atlantic City and Philadelphia clubs, he had produced shows for the Silver Slipper in New York, which was also owned by the Madden-DeMange group. In coming to the Cotton Club, he simply transferred to another branch of the corporation.

Healy was higly pleased with his Cotton Club assignment, for it allowed him unbridled exercise of his fast-stepping, up-tempo tastes in entertainment. "The chief ingredient was pace, pace, pace!" he later said, explaining his formula for the shows. "The show was generally built around types: the band, an eccentric dancer, a comedian—whoever we had who was also a star. The show ran an hour and a half, sometimes two hours; we'd break it up with a good voice . . . And we'd have a special singer who gave the

White literary rebels . . . saw Negroes not as people but as symbols of everything white America was not. The concept of the existence of a "New Negro" and the publicity given to it in the 1920's was primarily the result of this new awareness and interest in Negro society by what one writer called the "New White Man." The generation that discovered "newness" all around itself—New Humanism, New Thought, New Women, New Criticism, New Psychology, New Masses, New Poetry, New Science, New Era, New Words, New Morality and so on—also found a "New Negro."

—Gilbert Osofsky, Harlem: The Making of a Ghetto

customers the expected adult song in Harlem . . ."[3]

The acts themselves were only part of Healy's formula. Production was also important, and under Healy's direction the Cotton Club became probably the first night club to feature actual miniature stage sets and elaborate lighting as well as spectacular costumes.

Ever since the start of Prohibition, the mobster element had been extending its control over Harlem night life, and early in 1926 one of the holdouts, or pre-Prohibition night-club operators still in business, was dealt with in gangland fashion. Realizing that in order to keep his exclusive club open it was necessary to make some concessions to the various syndicates that had invaded Harlem, Barron Wilkins had for five or six years purchased his bootleg liquor from the gangsters. As one story goes, around late 1925 or early 1926 he received a shipment that he considered inferior and refused to pay for it. In response to such insubordination, the boys dispatched Yellow Charleston, a well-known junkie of the era, to deal with him. Early one morning in 1926, Charleston stabbed Wilkins in front of the Exclusive Club.

According to another story, Wilkins had refused to lend Charleston a trifling sum of money, and Charleston's act was individual and not mob-directed. Whatever the

New Year's Eve at the Cotton Club, 1938. (UPI)

reason, Barron Wilkins was killed, and shortly thereafter the Exclusive Club closed, to be reopened under new names and new management again and again but never to regain its former popularity. Although there is no proof that Madden's gang was directly involved in the elimination of Wilkins, and thus of his club, the loss of a major competitor did nothing to hurt the Cotton Club's business.

Sporadic outbreaks of gang violence occurred throughout the twenties, but underworld tensions and conflicts in New York did not compare to those in Al Capone's Chicago. When the St. Valentine's Day Massacre rocked Chicago in 1929, New York gangdom was enjoying relative peace, although that peace was shattered the following year.

Chapter 3

DUKE ELLINGTON COMES TO THE COTTON CLUB

Many who are familiar with Harlem—and music—history remember 1927 as the year singer Florence Mills died. It was a sudden, tragic occurrence. One week before, she had been feted at a "welcome home" banquet upon her triumphal return from Europe, and all Harlem mourned her passing in one of the most elaborate funerals in Harlem history. It was also the year when Andy Preer died, and when the Cotton Club found a new band that would make it famous.

Preer's group, the Missourians, or the Cotton Club Syncopators, was an average band; its entrée to the Cotton Club had been due chiefly to the fact that most of the members had played in and around Chicago or came from there. Without Preer they did not have sufficient drawing power, so the club's owners decided to bring in a new group.

Harry Block, the club's boss at the time, offered the spot to Joe (King) Oliver, whose Dixie Syncopators were just finishing up

Opposite: Duke Ellington. (Culver Pictures)

more than six years of gigs in Chicago. But the King turned down the offer—not enough money for a ten-piece band, he said. (This, when Cotton Club performers were the highest paid in Harlem.) The opening of the new show had already been postponed to December 4 because the club was without a band, so the turndown put Block in a quandary.

Jimmy McHugh, by then a veteran and respected member of the Cotton Club entertainment team, spoke up. He knew of a band, he said. It had been at the Kentucky Club in Times Square for a year and was now at a theater in Philadelphia. Duke Ellington and the Washingtonians played the kind of music McHugh wanted for the show.

At first McHugh's suggestion went unheeded. Ellington's band was out of

Washington, D.C.; it had never been near Chicago. While the tradition of hiring Chicagoans had been allowed to elapse with respect to waiters, cooks, busboys, and so forth, it was still strong when it came to hiring bands. But McHugh persisted, and Jack Johnson lent his support. Finally Block agreed to audition the Ellington band.

. . . the job [as Ellington would recall] . . . called for a band of at least eleven pieces, and we had been using only six at the Kentucky Club. At the time, I was playing a vaudeville show for Clarence Robinson at Gibson's Standard Theater on South Street in Philadelphia. The audition was set for noon, but by the time I had scraped up eleven men it was two or three o'clock. We played for them and got the job. The reason for that was that the boss, Harry Block, didn't get there till late either, and didn't hear the others! That's a classic example of being at the right place at the right time with the right thing before the right people.[1]

Block liked what he heard and signed a contract with Ellington's agent, Irving Mills. However, a new problem then presented itself. The band's contract to play at Gibson's Standard Theater in Philadelphia ran for a week beyond the date of the Cotton Club's planned opening, and Clarence Robinson firmly refused to release the band any earlier. In desperation, McHugh pleaded with the Madden people to do something. They did.

They called Boo Boo Hoff, a friend and a powerful underworld figure in Philadelphia. He in turn called Yankee Schwartz, who often acted as his emissary in such situations. "Be big," Schwartz advised Clarence Robinson, "or you'll be dead." With much haste the theater's management amended Ellington's contract.

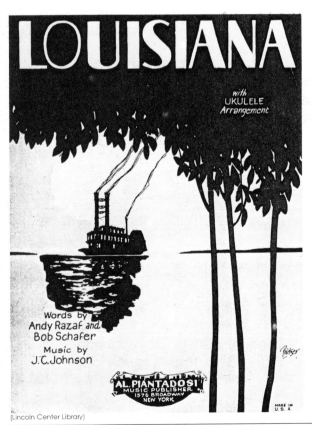

LOUISIANA

with UKULELE Arrangement

Words by Andy Razaf and Bob Schafer

Music by J.C. Johnson

AL. PIANTADOSI MUSIC PUBLISHER 1576 BROADWAY NEW YORK

MADE IN U.S.A.

(Lincoln Center Library)

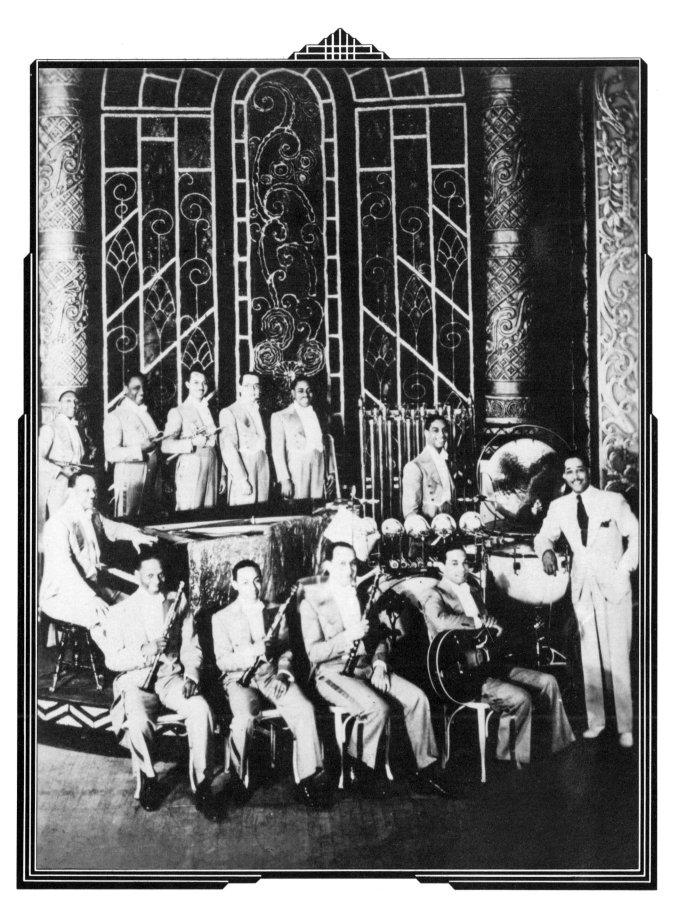

Ellington and his band finished their job in Philadelphia on the day of the Cotton Club's new opening. Then they headed north, arriving just minutes before show time. Tired and nervous, the band did not play well that opening night. The customers responded only politely, and Block complained to McHugh that Ellington's sound was too jangling and dissonant. McHugh chewed his nails and wondered when he would be given his walking papers.

Both Elllington and McHugh survived that opening night, and they could thank the black musicians of Harlem and the proprietor of "Mexico's" gin mill on 133rd Street for helping Ellington's band come through at the Cotton Club after a shaky beginning.

The musicians had begun to follow Duke Ellington and the Washingtonians when they first appeared at the Kentucky Club, and had followed it closely since then, buying its records, talking it up. When word came that Ellington was opening at the Cotton Club, the musicians increased their supportive efforts. So did "Mexico," who bet $100 and a hat that the Ellington band would make the grade. "Mexico's" real name was Gomez, and he came from South Carolina. His nickname derived from his service as a machine gunner with General Funston against Pancho Villa. He ran "the hottest gin mill in town" according to Harlem's musicians, and they spent hours at his place, drinking his "ninety-nine per cent": "One more degree either way would bust your top," Ellington used to say. At every opportunity Mexico praised the Ellington band, and the fact that he had bet so much on the Washingtonians

In the primitive world, where people live closer to the earth and much nearer to the stars, every inner and outer act combines to form the single harmony, life. Not just the tribal lore then, but every movement of life becomes a part of their education. They do not, as many civilized people do, neglect the truth of the physical for the sake of the mind. Nor do they teach with speech alone, but rather with all the acts of life. There are no books, so the barrier between words and reality is not so great as with us. The earth is right under their feet. The stars are never far away. The strength of the surest dream is the strength of the primitive world.

—Langston Hughes, The Big Sea

Duke Ellington and his famous Cotton Club orchestra. (Jazz Galleria)

inspired considerable respect. Mexico knew what he was talking about; Ellington's band would run a first gig of five years at the Cotton Club.

The strict color line at the club prevented the black musicians from showing their support in person, but they talked up the opening in all the uptown bars. Eventually the news crossed 110th Street and reached the ears of downtown white musicians, who traveled to Harlem to see what the talk was all about. The significance of their presence was not lost on the Cotton Club people. Before long, Duke Ellington and the Washingtonians were in tight. The Chicago-

oriented Cotton Club people became their greatest fans.

The Cotton Club show that had opened on December 4, 1927, was a long one, fifteen acts with a number of encores. Ellington's band usually led off with a show piece and played two or three numbers during the revue, almost always including their "Harlem River Quiver," which they had recorded on the Victor label. The bulk of the show was written by Jimmy McHugh, although for part of it he had a partner,

Above: Dorothy Fields and Jimmy McHugh.
(Collection of Duncan Schiedt)
Below: Duke Ellington. (Museum of the
City of New York)

Dorothy Fields. The McHugh-Fields team was destined to make musical history.

The twenty-three-year-old Miss Fields came by her talent naturally, for she was the daughter of Lew Fields of the famous Weber and Fields vaudeville and musical-comedy team. She did not, however, come by her profession easily, for Lew Fields was adamant about not letting any of his children become involved in the theater. Stubbornly Dorothy went her own way, working at whatever job she could find while writing songs and waiting for a break. (She got the idea for  Annie Get Your Gun while working as captain of the kitchen at the Stage Door Canteen. One of the dishwashers she supervised was Alfred Lunt.) Dorothy did not even tell her father when she took the opportunity to team up with composer McHugh; she knew he would violently oppose her association with a mobster-operated Harlem night club. In fact, she had misgivings about the situation herself, but as things turned out, she could not have chosen a physically safer place to begin her lyric-writing career.

"They were such gentlemen," she later said, referring to Stark, DeMange and company. "That was my first job as a lyric-writer, doing the Cotton Club shows with Jimmy McHugh. The owners were very solicitous of me; they grew furious when anyone used improper language in my presence . . . Stark took me up one day to see his prize pigeons. He lived over the club and kept the pigeons on the roof. He was very attached to them. He had become acquainted with pigeons in prison, when they had perched on the window sill of his cell. He had considered them his only friends there."[2]

With such accounts, Dorothy was able to convince her father that she was in no danger at the Cotton Club, and at the opening a proud Lew Fields was in the audience. He had brought Walter Winchell

along to observe his daughter's work, which in that first show consisted primarily of the lyrics to one song that was performed probably by Edith Wilson.

When it came time for the song, Dorothy looked over at her father and beamed with pride. She was certain the song would dissolve his reservations about her making a career in show business. But as the singer began the number, Dorothy flushed with anger and embarrassment. More than anything else, she wished her father were not there to hear it.

The singer had changed the lyrics. They were so dirty I blushed. I told Pop I was not the author. He went to the owner, who was a big gangster of the period, and told him that if he didn't announce that his daughter did not write those lyrics he would knock his block off. The gangster obliged. It was a poor start in show business.[3]

Nevertheless, Dorothy Fields remained in show business and at the Cotton Club, where she and McHugh produced some of the most famous songs in popular-music history.

The big numbers in that Cotton Club show were Dancemania and Jazzmania, and in them McHugh captured the essence of the attitude toward jazz of the day. Ellington and the band, however, supplied the rhythms and the instrumental voices that transmitted the "madness" to their audiences. Harry Carney on baritone sax, Rudy Jackson on tenor sax, Louis Metcalf on trumpet, and Wellman Braud, the bassman, all did their part. But it was the originals—Ellington, Toby Hardwick on alto

Chorus line. (Schomburg Collection, NYPL)

Duke Ellington Comes to the Cotton Club

saxophone, James (Bubber) Miley and Freddie Gay on trumpet, Joe Nanton on trombone and Sonny Greer on drums—who were most responsible for the band's exciting sound.

Greer and his drums provided the focus of the band's music. He had an incredible battery of percussion equipment, everything from tom-toms to snares to kettle drums, and once he realized the band was at the club to stay awhile, he brought in the really good stuff. He later recalled:

When we got into the Cotton Club, presentation became very important. I was a designer for the Leedy Manufacturing Company of Elkhart, Indiana, and the president of the company had a fabulous set of drums made for me, with timpani, chimes, vibraphone, everything. Musicians used to come to the Cotton Club just to see it. The value of it was three thousand dollars, a lot of money at that time, but it became an obsession with the racketeers, and they would pressure bands to have drums like mine, and would often advance money for them.[4]

With such equipment, Greer could make every possible drum sound, and at the Cotton Club he awed the customers, conjuring up tribal warriors and man-eating tigers

and war dancers. But his rhythms were only the focus of the band's sound. Every section contributed its own finely tuned, finely rehearsed part of the jungle sound, and the sections blended together so well that it was hard to distinguish the individual elements. Paul Whiteman and his arranger, Fred Grofe, visited the Cotton Club nightly for more than a week but finally admitted that they could not steal even two bars of the amazing music.

The featured Cotton Club singers and dancers completed the exotic image. Earl "Snakehips" Tucker could twist his haunches and thigh joints into unbelievable contortions. He was called a human boa constrictor and became an immediate sensation. Edith Wilson wore an abbreviated costume and did slapstick comedy in addition to singing the "adult songs" which Healy's formula called for. The dancing team of Mildred and Henri regaled the audience with their intricate steps. Watching and listening to the spectacle, the Cotton Club patrons could have no doubt that

While Harlem supper clubs catering to whites flourished, public schools did not teach black children about electricity "because they couldn't get licenses anyway."

Opposite: Earl "Snakehips" Tucker, 1925.
(Schomburg Collection NYPL)

they were witnessing firsthand the emergence of the primal African from beneath the sequined costumes and tan skins of the performers.

Within a few weeks the band was no longer known as the Washingtonians but as Duke Ellington's Jungle Band. While many of Ellington's titles from this period reflect the "jungle" motif—"Jungle Jamboree," "Jungle Blues," "Jungle Nights in Harlem," "Echoes of the Jungle"—such titles were conceived as attention- and publicity-getters by Ellington's agent, Irving Mills, and had little to do with Ellington or the compositions themselves. Ellington had mixed feelings about this "Jungle Band" reputation; he was not simply catering to white tastes. "As a student of Negro history I had, in any case, a natural inclination in this direction," he would later say. As a matter of fact, the growl style which the Ellington orchestra developed to perfection is simply a development of the "vocalization" of instrumental tone and inflection which is so characteristic of black music.

The average Cotton Club patron would not have understood this—or cared to. What the average customer wanted was exciting, dazzling jazz, and that is what the Ellington band gave them. In the process, Ellington and his men sometimes slipped into a manner of playing that was patronizing and uninvolved, for they hadn't the opportunity to play the fierce, creative music that the bands played at the Savoy, or the Nest Club, or Small's Paradise, where there was a larger black audience. Still, even playing before an audience not knowledgeable in the subtleties of jazz, there were times when the band members achieved an intimacy and a unity of feeling that could never again be duplicated.

It is said that once the entire brass section of the band rose and played such an intricate and beautiful chorus that the usually poised and dignified Eddie Duchin actually rolled under the table in ecstasy.

Despite the lack of creative opportunities, Ellington welcomed the upturn that his career had taken since his arrival at the Cotton Club. And he had the club to thank for the upturn in his personal life, too. At the Cotton Club Duke Ellington had fallen in love.

It was not the first time for the amorous Duke, nor would it be the last, but at the time he was free; he had broken up with his wife, Edna Thompson Ellington. He and Edna, who was also a musician, had been high school sweethearts in Washington. They were married in 1918 and not long after, their son, Mercer, was born. A child born later died in infancy. When Ellington decided to go to New York in 1922, Edna followed him. The first years were happy and exciting, but as time went on, the two grew apart, and while they continued to love each other very much, they realized they had nothing in common. Reluctantly

"Snakehips" Tucker and Evelyn Welch.
(Collection of Duncan Schiedt)

Duke Ellington Comes to the Cotton Club

Duke Ellington, at far left. (Jazz Galleria)

they broke up, and Edna went back home, taking little Mercer with her.

With Edna gone, Duke felt his aloneness keenly, and his eye for beautiful young women, always acute, sharpened even more. December 4, 1927, the night Ellington's band opened at the Cotton Club, was also the opening night for Mildred Dixon, who was teamed in a dancing duo with Henri Wessells. Short, sleek and dark-eyed, she attracted Duke's interest immediately, and it is likely that one reason for the band's poor performance that opening night was Duke's preoccupation with the beautiful dancer.

"Since he played with his feet well in front of him," biographer Barry Ulanov reported in 1946, "and with his face turned to the audience, if he got interested in something other than the music, he could always fake the chords, just run his hands deftly over the keys and make it look right, even if he weren't playing a note. He faked the first time he saw Mildred."[5]

Duke and Mildred got acquainted—during rehearsals, and after Duke felt secure in his position at the Cotton Club, during shows. She was interested in what he was doing and what he was feeling, and he found himself trusting and confiding in her. Shortly thereafter Mildred left show business to become the second Mrs. Ellington.

Mildred Dixon was not the only girl in the Cotton Club show to pair up with a member of the Washingtonians. Soon after the band went into the club, drummer Sonny Greer married Millicent Cook and took her out of the chorus line.

Meanwhile the band and the club were on their way to national fame. WHW, a small local radio station, began to broadcast a nightly session of Ellington's music

from the Cotton Club, and it was not long
before both band and club got a fantastic
break. Columbia Broadcasting System, represented by its famous announcer Ted Husing, approached Herman Stark with the
idea of broadcasting the sessions on a
national basis.

Stark was cool to Husing. "There's no
money in it for me. It will do you some
good, not me. However, it'll probably do
Duke some good, too, so go ahead and
we'll see what happens."[6]

What happened was that the "Cotton
Club sound" became a national smash.
Before long, nearly every American who
had a radio knew of the Cotton Club, and
what visions of glamour and sophistication
and big-city wickedness that name con-
jured up in their minds! A trip to Harlem,
and to the Cotton Club in particular,
became a "must" for every Midwesterner
who visited New York City. Tourists from all
over the country came flocking uptown.

Within a year Ellington had become such
a prize property that the Cotton Club
agreed to his request to relax the "whites
only" policy. This is not to say that Ellington
pushed for complete integration of the clientele, or that the club suddenly welcomed black patrons. But Ellington had
hinted that it was a shame some of his
friends could not enter the club to hear
him and that the families of the other performers were not permitted to watch them.
The management, aware of its stake in
Ellington, had cautiously acceded, at least
while he was at the club. But black customers were still carefully examined before
being admitted. The complexion of the
Cotton Club audience did not change
radically; after all, there were not that
many Harlemites who cared to patronize
the new semi–Jim Crow establishment.

The white "slummers" continued to
come in droves. They spent their money
lavishly, for it was a time of heavy investing
in the stock market, and of premium divi-
dends. Many whites threw their money
around "like there was no tomorrow,"
much to the glee of the club's staff and

> Sometimes when I'm lonely.
> Don't know why,
> Keep thinkin' I won't be lonely
> By and by
>
> —Langston Hughes

Duke Ellington Comes to the Cotton Club

entertainers. Waiters hardly even considered their $1 per night salary when they spoke of their gross earnings per week. It was the tips that made life beautiful, particularly for those waiters with facility in popping champagne corks with aplomb.

The entertainers fared even better. As a member of the Cotton Club band, Sonny Greer made $45 per week in salary. However, there were ways of augmenting that quite respectable wage. "Anytime we needed a quick buck, we would push the piano up next to the table of the biggest racketeer in the joint. I would then sing 'My Buddy' to him. I never remember getting less than a $20 tip for such an easy five minutes' work."[7] Drunks were even easier to manipulate. "You're in Harlem now," the table singer would tell one. "You can't give my piano player a little old dollar bill." Naturally, the drunk would make proper amends.

"It didn't really matter what the salary was," Duke Ellington later remarked. "A big bookmaker like Meyer Boston would come in late and the first thing he'd do was change $20 into half dollars. Then he'd throw the whole thing at the feet of whoever was singing or playing or dancing. If you've ever heard $20 in halves land on a wooden floor you know what a wonderful sound it makes."[8]

The Ellington band was making good money and getting the exposure so necessary for success. The members of the band were grateful to the Cotton Club for such opportunities and they were also quite happy at the club. They became friends with the regular Cotton Club performers, dated the girls, and sometimes married them. They also became friends with the members of the Madden gang and their associates. Owney Madden rarely presented himself at the club, preferring private parties in his penthouse apartment in Chelsea, not far from his Phoenix Central Cereal Beverage Company. In fact, he rarely left his apartment, and when he did he always rode in his bulletproof Duesenberg. However, when the Duesenberg did roll up in front of the Cotton Club, and Madden entered, escorted by his bodyguards, he was always polite, and as the members of the Ellington band would put it, straight.

"I keep hearing how bad the gangsters were," Sonny Greer said later. "All I can say is that I wish I was still working for them.

At that time colored people realized that their instinctive sense of values was more elegant than ours, and they were tolerant of us.

—Anita Loos, A Girl Like I

Their word was all you needed. They had been brought up with the code that you either kept your word or you got dead."[9]

Big French DeMange was a particular fan of Ellington's music and of Ellington himself. "Anything you want, Duke," Frenchy liked to say, "anything you want you ask for it, and it's yours," and there was no question that Big Frenchy DeMange could make good on his offer.

Frenchy loved to play cards, and often after the 2 A.M. show he and Stark and Duke and Mildred would play cards until the sun came up. First they would play whist, then pinochle, and finally, as the boys from the kitchen served their breakfast, rummy, which was easiest to play while eating and drinking. Then they would adjourn to their respective homes or quarters and go to bed.

Other evenings Duke would go alone or with some of his band members to one of the speakeasies on "the Corner," 131st Street and Seventh Avenue. During the twenties and early thirties, this was the site of the most creative music-making in Harlem. Connie's Inn was located there. Connie Immerman welcomed the black musicians in the early-morning hours after they finished their stints in other clubs, and gangster Dutch Schultz showed he was more musically hip than the Madden gang by hanging out there frequently. The Band Box Club at 161 West 131st Street, run by cornetist Addington Major, was another favorite gathering place. It had no regular musical program, but plenty of music was made there. Its special rear bar became one of the most popular places for jam sessions. The Barbecue, the rib joint in Harlem, also had no regular live music. It was the first place in Harlem to have a juke box, although the new contraption really wasn't

needed. The counter was directly over the bandstand downstairs in Connie's Inn.

Monday mornings about five o'clock, it was customary for Cotton Club performers to go next door and upstairs to the Lenox Club, on Lenox Avenue and 144th Street, for the weekly breakfast dance. Almost every big-time act in town would be there to do its number, and it was not unusual to see Bill Robinson, Ethel Waters, Louis Armstrong, Duke Ellington and Cab Calloway (who did not have his own band yet) all in one morning. In such places, Duke and the other musicians from clubs like the Cotton Club that were out of the jazz mainstream could get down to real jazz and find stimulation from other experimenters in the medium.

Chapter 4

THE DEPRESSION BEGINS

 On October 23, 1929, the first blow fell on the reckless prosperity of America. The New York Stock Exchange witnessed a minor panic among stocks that speculators had pushed to fantastic heights. The next day, "Black Thursday," saw rampant hysteria. Rumors of mass suicides attracted a crowd of spectators to Wall Street to scan the windows of the tall buildings and to gather under a scaffolding to watch an ordinary workman in morbid expectation of his plunge. Five days later, on the 29th, America realized that the 23rd had represented merely the initial, warning tremors of the crash.

American optimism did not crash along with Wall Street. The stiff-upper-lip tradition prevailed and, indeed, became official policy. New York mayor Jimmy Walker requested that movie theaters show only cheerful films. The message, "Forward America, Nothing Can Stop U.S.," appeared on billboards across the nation. The song "Happy Days Are Here Again" was copyrighted on November 7.

Opposite: Ethel Waters impersonating Josephine Baker. (Culver Pictures)

Publicity photo of the <u>Hot Chocolates</u> of 1936.
(Author's collection)

Up in Harlem, the clubs rocked as tipsily as before. Connie's Inn was entering its peak period. Louis Armstrong, with Carroll Dickerson's orchestra in from Chicago, were attracting turn-away crowds to their <u>Hot Chocolates</u> show. By this time Armstrong was really in the money, and he dressed accordingly. Clarinetist Mezz Mezzrow later described his and Armstrong's dress when they went out on the town: "... oxford-gray, double-breasted suits, white silk-broadcloth shirts (Louis wore Barrymore collars for comfort when he played, with great big knots in his ties), black double-breasted, velvet-collared overcoats, formal white silk mufflers, French lisle hand-clocked socks, black custom-built London brogues, white silk handkerchiefs tucked in the breast pockets of our suits, a derby for Louis, a light gray felt for me with the brim turned down on one side, kind of debonair and rakish."[1] Over at the Cotton Club, Duke Ellington and his band played as gaily as ever, for their careers were skyrocketing. In 1929 they appeared simultaneously at the Cotton Club and in Ziegfeld's <u>Show Girl</u>, for which Gershwin had written the score and which introduced "An American in Paris" and "Liza." In 1930 they first accompanied Maurice Chevalier at the Fulton Theatre and later in the summer traveled to Hollywood to appear in <u>Check and Double Check</u>, a film featuring the popular radio team of Amos 'n Andy. As the latter gig could not be managed simultaneously with nightly stands at the Cotton Club, another band was hired to fill in . . .

"I was with the band in a little spot down on Broadway, the Crazy Cat Club, and they found me down there and demanded that I come to the Cotton Club the next day,"[2]

Cab Calloway. (Culver Pictures)

and Calloway went on to sing, first with Louis Armstrong's Chicago band, and then with Marion Hardy's Alabamians, a band in Chicago that included trumpeter Eddie Mallory and bassist Charlie "Fat Man" Turner.

In the winter of 1928–1929, the band traveled to New York to play at the Savoy Ballroom. While there, Calloway and Hardy fought so bitterly about who was to be billed as leader that when the Savoy contract was up, the two split. The Alabamians went to Connie's Inn, and Calloway himself was temporarily out of a band.

This situation was not to last for long. Irving Mills, Calloway's agent as well as Duke Ellington's, suggested that Calloway team up with Andy Preer's old band. Calloway needed a band, and the Missourians, who had done little since leaving the Cotton Club, needed an exciting leader.

Calloway was that, and in fact at first he was something of a shock to the veteran band members. From the first downbeat to the last note of a number, he was all motion. He waved his arms, he ran back and forth from orchestra to microphone, he danced in a frenzy to the music. His hair flew one way, his coattails another. The first time the Missourians played with him they were so startled at his performance that it's amazing they missed no notes. Cab Calloway in action was really something to see.

The audience loved it. The tension—wondering whether or not he was going to crash into the band or the microphone—only heightened the excitement of watching him perform. Once he actually fell off a stage and broke his ankle.

Cab Calloway changed the Missourians from a background orchestra to an act in their own right, and Irving Mills had little trouble booking them into the Cotton Club as a replacement for Ellington's band. The club's popularity continued undiminished

Cab Calloway recently recalled. It was a great opportunity for the band to follow Ellington at the Cotton Club, although the spot was already familiar to many of the band's members, who had played at the club as Andy Preer's Missourians.

Calloway, who was born in Rochester, New York, had begun his musical career in Chicago, where he worked as a drummer while studying pre-law at Chicago's Crane College. Playing in the South Side clubs attracted him much more than his studies,

despite Ellington's absence, for Calloway was a one-man attraction. Lucky for Calloway that he was so popular with audiences, including the Cotton Club patrons; otherwise his first engagement at the club might well have been his last. He pulled an historic boner on, of all nights, a Sunday, a "celebrity night," broadcast all over the area. As a Chicago columnist recalled the incident:

Healy had a benefit to play one Sunday night . . . But Dan couldn't get up to the Cotton Club for his usual stint, so the introductory task fell to the lot of the band leader, Cab Calloway. This was Cab's first engagement at the Cotton Club, and he hadn't acquired the savoir faire and the ability to ad lib which came to him in later years of experience at a microphone.

On this particular evening one of the world's most famous and beloved songwriters, Irving Berlin, was a guest at the club. He rarely was, or is, seen in night clubs and always has had the reputation of being a retiring, shy individual who shuns spotlights and anything savoring of notoriety or acclaim. His sincere modesty never has been questioned.

At his table were Oscar Levant, a pianist who frequently was Berlin's companion in that era, and Mrs. Levant. Mrs. Berlin, the former Ellin MacKay, never was seen with her husband on his own infrequent appearances in night spots.

A list of the guests present was prepared on cards by the head waiter, the captains and others, as usual, and presented to Calloway for his guidance in making the introductions. Cab got along fine for the first few moments, even slipping in a typical Healy compliment to someone's talent now and then.

Then he introduced Mr. and Mrs. Irving Berlin!

Necks craned in all directions, because the professional crowd there never had seen Mrs. Berlin in public. The head waiter and the captains got frantic, and Herman Stark, the manager, came charging out of his private office.

Throughout the speakeasy era, and for years after, the pleasure-lovers rarely considered the evening's excitement exhausted unless the night, or rather the early post-midnight hours were topped off with a journey into Harlem. We invaded the so-called Black Belt fearlessly and joyously, and regarded the welcome we received as warm and sincere. No one gave a thought in those earlier years to racial discord, to civil rights, or for that matter, paid too much attention to the difference in color, for we mingled on friendly terms, whites and blacks, in the diversion spots.

—Louis Sobol, The Longest Street

Before they could signal His Highness of Hi-de-ho, he already had introduced Oscar Levant at Berlin's table, and neither of them would arise to acknowledge the introduction.

Finally Kid Griffin, the suave custodian of the portals, called Calloway to the side of the floor and slipped him a card rectifying the error.

Cab returned to the microphone and apologized to his audience, to the listeners on the air as well as to the other guests in the club.

"It seems I made a very serious error in my last introduction," he explained.

"The lady with Mr. Berlin is not his wife!"

That halted the broadcast and the introductions for the evening. Dan Healy came back the following Sunday night.[3]

Ellington and his band returned to the Cotton Club early in 1930, after finishing their stint in Hollywood with Amos 'n Andy's Check and Double-Check. As Calloway

and his band had been hired merely to fill in while Ellington was away, naturally they were expected to leave and find another job. However, they were not expected to go to a rival club, and when they were signed on at the Plantation Club, the Cotton Club people were highly displeased.

The Plantation Club, at West 126th Street near Lenox Avenue, was an uptown branch of the successful Plantation Club on Broadway at Fiftieth Street, where Florence Mills, among other stars, had been featured. It was no secret that the uptown Plantation Club had been opened to draw away some of the Cotton Club's lucrative business. Calloway had done very well for the Cotton Club, and it was hoped that some of Calloway's fans would follow him to the Plantation sixteen blocks farther downtown.

One night the Plantation had unexpected and uninvited guests. "Some of the boys" smashed chairs and tables, shattered glasses and bottles, uprooted the bar and planted it on the curb outside. They reduced the place to such a shambles that it took months of work and thousands of dollars to put it back together. While no one around town cared to be quoted about the incident, word was out that Owney Madden's gang just might have had something to do with it. Early one morning a few weeks later, Harry Block's bullet-riddled body was found in the elevator of his apartment building. Although it was never proved, the story was that Block's murder was a direct result of the wrecking of the Plantation Club, which never did reopen in its original form.

In 1930 Jimmy McHugh and Dorothy Fields left the Cotton Club to go on to major prominence. While at the club, they had done other work on the side. In late

BANDANNA BABIES

LEW LESLIE'S

BLACKBIRDS of 1928

with UKULELE ARRANGEMENT

I CAN'T GIVE YOU ANYTHING BUT LOVE
DIG A DIG A DO
DOIN' THE NEW LOW-DOWN
SHUFFLE YOUR FEET AND ROLL ALONG
BANDANNA BABIES
HERE COMES MY BLACKBIRD
DIXIE
BABY
PORGY

Lyrics by DOROTHY FIELDS *Music by* JIMMY McHUGH

JACK MILLS

MADE IN U.S.A.

(Lincoln Center Library)

Ruth Etting visiting Ted Koehler and Harold Arlen at Columbia Studios, where the two songwriters are engaged in writing the music and lyrics for "Let's Fall in Love." (Culver Pictures)

1927 they had produced "I Can't Give You Anything But Love" which became a hit in Lew Leslie's Blackbirds of 1928 on Broadway, and in 1930 they were doing the score for The International Revue. In succeeding years they wrote such well-known songs as "On the Sunny Side of the Street, "I'm in the Mood for Love," "Lovely to Look At" and "Don't Blame Me." While they were grateful to the Cotton Club for helping to give them their start, both McHugh and Fields were glad to leave. Despite the solicitous treatment she received, Dorothy Fields in particular had frequently been dis-

gruntled there and had often refused to sign her name to some of the more "earthy" songs she was expected to do.

Their successors at the club felt much the same way and refused to allow many of the adult songs they were required to write to be either recorded or copyrighted. Harold Arlen, composer, and Ted Koehler, lyricist, had already become popular as the producers of the song "Get Happy," introduced by Ruth Etting in The 9:15 Revue in 1930. Like Dan Healy, they came to the Cotton Club from the downtown Madden-controlled spot the Silver Slipper. Healy

needed songwriters for the club's fall 1930 show, Brown Sugar—Sweet, But Unrefined, and Arlen and Koehler were available, so they signed on at a salary of $50 a week plus all the food they could eat. The salary was meager, but the two songwriters were happy to have the chance to write for a club whose productions were as close to Broadway as one could get without actually being on the Great White Way.

Clearly, there is no such thing as a "winning" songwriting method. Each individual and each team of songwriters has a particular style, but Arlen and Koehler's, especially Koehler's, was so casual and

Cab Calloway, the hi-de-ho man, whooping it up.
(Collection of Duncan Schiedt)

matter-of-fact that it is difficult to realize what thought and talent went into the works they produced. Usually Arlen would begin the process by writing a rough draft of the music. Then he would go to the piano and play it, over and over, polishing it. Meanwhile Koehler would be stretched out on a couch, listening, thinking. Sometimes he would appear to doze and Arlen, feeling he was working harder than his partner, would shout at him to wake him up. Immediately Koehler would snap to attention, tapping his feet and whistling to prove he was listening. As time went on, Arlen came to realize that Koehler was indeed working, for the completed lyric was always perfect for the tune. Koehler's theory was that lyrics came naturally and would not work if they were contrived. He simply didn't believe in "wasting his cells."

Among other physical activities in which Koehler did not like to engage was walking, although sometimes Arlen was able to talk him into doing so. One day in the winter of 1930–1931, Arlen persuaded Koehler to walk from the Croyden Hotel on Madison Avenue and Eighty-sixth Street, where Arlen lived, down to their publishers' office in midtown. The air was chilly, and before long Koehler began to complain and to make suggestions like "Why don't you join the Army if you love to walk so much?" Laughing at his friend's complaints, Arlen began to hum a marching tune, and in spite of himself Koehler fell into step and into the mood. By the time they reached Forty-seventh Street, "I Love a Parade" was nearly written.

By the end of 1930 the Cotton Club life had begun to pall for Duke Ellington. He felt cramped in his style. He was tired of playing show tunes. He had to admit that the people at the Cotton Club were good

about letting the band off to play outside gigs, but he needed a real change. He needed to get back in touch with his music. He and his band left the club.

Cab Calloway's band took over as the Cotton Club band, apparently harboring no hard feelings about the forced termination of their stint at the ill-fated Plantation Club. Just prior to coming back to the Cotton Club, they had played a very successful gig at the Alhambra Ballroom, breaking all former attendance records at the spot. Also, they had recently recorded the first of their big successes, "St. James Infirmary," with Brunswick Records. For old Missourians

such as trumpeters R. O. Dickerson, Lamar Wright and Reuben Reeves, trombonists DePriest Wheeler and Harry White, saxophonists Billy Blue, Andy Brown and Walter Thomas, pianist Earl Prince, banjoist Charley Stamps, bassist Jimmy Smith, and drummer LeRoy Maxey, it was about time. Compared with them, Calloway was a relative newcomer, but he welcomed this, the band's first extended engagement at the Cotton Club as much as they did. And well he might have, for it proved the real "making" of Calloway and his band.

The Cotton Club management hired Clarence Robinson to create and stage

Cab Calloway and band at the Cotton Club, 1932.
(Culver Pictures)

Cab Calloway and band at the Cotton Club, 1938.
(Culver Pictures)

The Depression Begins

Opposite: Aida Ward. (Collection of Duncan Schiedt)

New Year's Eve at the Cotton Club with Cab Calloway. (UPI)

the spring 1931 show. Apparently there also existed no hard feelings on Robinson's part over the "muscle" the Madden gang had used to get him to release Ellington and his band from their contract at Gibson's Standard Theater in Philadelphia back in 1927. What made his employment particularly notable was that it was the first time the job was given to a black. The show, Rhythmania, opened in March and was the most successful to date. It included Arlen and Koehler's "I Love a Parade," for which Healy devised a spectacular routine complete with batons and fancy stepping. Blues singer Aida Ward introduced their song "Between the Devil and the Deep Blue Sea," and Cab Calloway's specialties were "Trickeration" and "Kickin' the Gong

Around" which, with "Between the Devil and the Deep Blue Sea," were among the year's hits. In night-club history, however, this show would be overshadowed by the club's fall revue that year. It was the second 1931 show which catapulted Calloway to fame.

On the whole, there was nothing particularly memorable about the show. Cora LaRedd did her famous trick dancing, and Swan and Lee contributed their intricate team steps. Aida Ward and Leitha Hill sang their traditional torch songs. Arlen and Koehler's work was respectable but not particularly exciting. The real hit of the show was a number written and performed by Calloway in his own inimitable style. "Minnie the Moocher," a "low-down, hootchie-cootcher," practically became a folk character.

"My manager, Irving Mills, and I were sitting around the old Cotton Club in New York tossing phrases at each other," Calloway later recalled, "and 'Minnie the Moocher' came up. We banged out the lyrics and melody on the spot and tried it out a couple nights later. It went over big." That is an understatement. The night the song was introduced, the Cotton Club audience demanded six encores!

"Sometime after that," Calloway continued, "I didn't have my mind on my work while I was on the bandstand and in the middle of 'Minnie' I forgot the lyrics, so I yelled 'hi-de-ho' instead and the band took it up and then the customers. Out of that song I got a hit tune, a big-selling record, an offer of better jobs and a trade mark—'hi-de-ho.' "[4]

The band became known as the "hi-de-ho" band, and for the next twenty years Calloway was known as the "hi-de-ho" man.

To Yvonne,
Best Wishes,
From,
Aida Ward
"One of Blackbirds 1926"
London.

Hi-de-ho. It was merely a scatting of a song's lyrics, but it expressed the feeling of the times, the reckless gaiety of a society that refused to recognize that the economic bottom had fallen through. Anyone reading the society columns or frequenting the night spots would find it hard to believe that a Depression was going on. The dancers moved with the same abandon, and the conversation was as animated as ever. These young gadabouts, these wealthy white patrons, these favored black entertainers had not yet been touched by the Depression. They danced on, carried the momentum of earlier prosperity. For them the twenties had passed into the thirties rather smoothly, and they saw no reason to greet the new decade with any other attitude than the cynical, worldy abandon with which they had related to the old. That year, 1931, saw the opening of the world's finest luxury hotel, the new Waldorf-Astoria. The tallest building in the world, the Empire State Building, was completed. In the same year the architects' plans for Rockefeller Center were published. The entertainment industry as a whole did not feel the effects of the crash for some time. In fact, initially, it benefited. People turned to commercial entertainment to help them forget their troubles or to help delay the realization of their troubles. The hit song of 1931 was "Life Is Just a Bowl of Cherries," and nothing epitomized that attitude more than the nightly mood at the Cotton Club.

The club had become the favorite late-night spot of the fast set, which in those pre-jet days was called the Mink Set. Financier Otto Kahn was often there, as was Mayor Jimmy Walker (the club was officially on the mayor's Reception Committee list and was famed for its foreign visitors); show-business personalities, bankers, Texas cattle barons, the youngsters of both old and new monied families. They gave class to the Cotton Club, which gave them social standing in return. Opening nights at the club were as exciting and celebrity-stud-

They camel and fish-tail and turkey, they geche and black bottom and scronch, they skate and buzzard and mess-around—and they do them all better than I!

—Rudolph Fisher, "The Caucasian Storms Harlem"

Floor show from the famous Harlem night club "The Cotton Club," featuring a leggy row of chorus girls. Photograph 1920s. (Bettmann Archive)

ded as any Broadway premiere. All the important columnists were there, men like Walter Winchell and Louis Sobol and Ed Sullivan. Americans across the country sat glued to their radios, listening to Ted Husing's coverage of the events just as, later, Americans would sit transfixed at their television sets watching the Academy Awards.

The show people who came uptown after an evening entertaining an audience to be entertained themselves were frequently asked to contribute their talents on an impromptu basis. One of Dan Healy's cleverest ideas was to inaugurate Sunday "celebrity nights," and on a given Sunday evening one was quite likely to see Marilyn Miller do a soft-shoe, or Helen Morgan sing a tearful song. On Sunday night the Cotton

Club Girls wore their best finery and paraded past the celebrities' tables after the show, hoping to be noticed. Invariably, they were. Like the waiters, the Cotton Club Girls played their role to the hilt, exuding an aura of glamour, living proof of the club's advertisement—"Tall, Tan and Terrific."

Adam Clayton Powell, Jr., sufficiently light-complexioned to gain admittance to the Cotton Club even in the early days, met his first wife, Isabel Washington, when she was a Cotton Club Girl. Adelaide Marshall met her wealthy husband at the club. At least three other girls did the same, but were so light-skinned that they passed into white society.

On Sunday nights a number of young hopefuls who would frequent any celebrity

spot where there was a possibility of being "discovered" could be found at the Cotton Club. Powell recalled in his autobiography:

. . . I remember sitting in the Cotton Club when it was uptown and owned by the mob. A keen-looking, handsome fellow was hanging around in those days. He was a friend of but not part of the mob that controlled the underworld of New York. He was interested in show business but couldn't seem to get anywhere at that time, and in order to pick up a quarter here and there, and to bask in the lights of glamour, he hung around the Cotton Club. One night backstage I asked him to go out and get something for one of the girls, and when he came back I gave him a half dollar. His name was George Raft.[5]

Money flowed as freely at the Cotton Club as "Madden's No. 1" beer. The club's philosophy was: We spare no expense for the comfort of our customers, and our customers spare no expense to have a good time. To pay for the forty entertainers in the lavish shows, staged at an average weekly cost of $4,000, the club charged exorbitant prices by the average person's standards, beginning with a $2.50 cover charge. At $1, a bottle of Madden's beer was quite reasonable, and the prices of mixers encouraged customers to order it, or discouraged them from drinking the liquor they had brought with them. A glass of orange juice cost $1.25, a quart of lemonade $3.50, a tiny bottle of ginger ale cost $1. Even milk was 50 cents.

Food prices were comparable to those in other cabarets. A steak sandwich was $1.25, as was the plate of scrambled eggs and sausage. Lobster and crabmeat cocktails could be ordered for $1. A side order of olives was 50 cents. The Chinese soups were all 50 cents each, and the most expensive Chinese main dish, Moo Goo Guy Pan, was $2.25. While the Cotton Club

did not net a lot from its sale of food, its cover charge and beverage sales produced a healthy profit, which was fortunate for the Madden people, who once found it necessary to pay out a large portion of those profits to ransom Big Frenchy.

About 1930 occurred the first real trouble among the gangsters that was to lead to the end of the Harlem era. While Owney Madden controlled the bootleg business in Manhattan, the Bronx business was in the hands of Arthur Flegenheimer, more widely known as Dutch Schultz. One of Schultz's lieutenants was a young man named Coll. The story goes that Schultz and Coll had a falling-out and Coll was "hit" by Schultz's men. Coll's younger brother, Vincent, better known as "The Mick," determined to avenge his brother's death. He hit a couple of Schultz's men and then boldly announced that he was merely working his way up to the top.

The New York underworld was unprepared for the likes of Vincent Coll. Certainly they were no strangers to murder, but it was of the orderly kind, involving conferences and votes and contracts. Vincent Coll defied all the rules. It was not long before "The Mick" became known as "Mad Dog." Then "Mad Dog" went too far. Gunning for another of Schultz's men on a Harlem street, he killed a five-year-old boy instead and wounded other children as they played. He made front-page headlines as "The Baby Killer," and then the police were after him.

Up against both the mob and the law, "Mad Dog" grew desperate. He'd attracted a fairly large coterie of reckless young hoods, so he didn't lack manpower. What he needed was money, and in one of the boldest moves in New York gangland history, he kidnapped George "Big Frenchy" DeMange and George Immerman, Connie (Connie's Inn) Immerman's brother, and held them for ransom.

"He was looking to snatch me," Connie Immerman later reported, "but I wasn't in the joint that night and they took George instead. It was funny about The Mick. He phoned me and assured me that George was all right. He said that George had some money on him, that it would be taken, and George would be released. But I was to get together the difference between what George had and $20,000 and have it ready with the doorman at Connie's on a certain night."[6]

Meanwhile DeMange sent word to Madden that Coll wanted a higher sum, $35,000 according to one story, $50,000 by another, for his return. Madden paid. Both hostages were released, and the corpulent Frenchy's return to the Cotton Club was an occasion of great celebration.

The safe return of George and Frenchy did not end the matter, which was the way of some gangster troubles. Wars between mobs often ended in a truce, and differences were theoretically forgotten. But when one of the combatants was an individual, and one who did not play by the rules at that, the end was more direct and final. In 1932 "Mad Dog" Coll was ambushed in a telephone booth on Twenty-Third Street in New York's Chelsea district by two machine-gun-packing lieutenants of Dutch Schultz.

The incident had no effect on the Cotton Club's business. It had taken place away from the club and did not directly involve it. Most of the patrons never even knew about what had happened. In view of the club's management, it is surprising that there were never any typically gangland incidents at the club in the mobster's heyday that was Prohibition.

In 1932 another of the rigid color standards maintained at the Cotton Club was relaxed—the one governing selection of Cotton Club Girls. The "whites only" admission policy had been eased some four years earlier, enabling relatives and friends of performers as well as important blacks to enter, although they were frequently seated at back tables near the kitchen. The policy of hiring only light-complexioned chorus girls—"nothing darker than a light olive tint"—had seemed unassailable. Yet in 1932 Lucille Wilson did challenge it, and she won. She displayed talent and guts during her audition and charmed Harold Arlen, among others. The Cotton

In 1935 racial discrimination in downtown New York City was such that Marian Anderson could not get a hotel room.

To Hy.
One of my very
best friends. Wish-
ing you the be—
always.
Sincerely
Lucille
Cotton Club.
2/8/40

Opposite: Lucille Wilson, 1940. (Author's collection)

Club management, challenged to come up with a rational reason why they should not at least give her a try, failed to do so.

Lucille Wilson was hired on a trial basis. If the customers complained, she was out. But the customers did not complain, and Lucille, who later became Mrs. Louis Armstrong, remained with the Cotton Club for eight years.

In 1932, there was also an increase in the number of rent parties in Harlem. A peculiarly Harlem institution, rent parties had begun when the busy war industries lured Southern blacks to New York City and slick landlords realized these newcomers would pay the most exorbitant rents in order to have a place to stay. Now that the Depression was on, paying the rent became an even greater struggle. Practically wherever one went in Harlem one was amused or beguiled by countless hand-lettered announcements promising good food and fine entertainment in return for a contribution to the monthly rent bill. While part of the money taken in went to pay for entertainment and refreshments, a successful rent party usually took care of the rent, and sometimes there was a little money left over.

Arlen and Koehler, particularly Arlen, were sensitive to the world outside the Cotton Club, and they quite frequently recorded local cultural traits in their songs. Partly this practice was good business, for the club's patrons were curious about the world of Harlem and responded to songs that seemed to give them an "inside look" at that world. But partly, too, these songs were an expression of Arlen's real feeling for Harlem and its people. They struck a responsive chord in the soul of this man born Hyman Arluck in Buffalo, New York, the son of a cantor.

Ethel Waters is supposed to have called him "the Negro-ist white man" she had ever known. Songwriter Roger Edens recalled going with Arlen to the Cotton Club and watching him rehearse with the cast:

He was really one of them. He had absorbed so much from them—their idiom, their tonalities, their phrasings, their rhythms—he was able to establish a warming rapport with them. The Negroes in New York at that time were possibly not as sensitive about themselves as they are today. But even so, they had a fierce insularity and dignity within themselves that resented the so-called "professional Southernism" that was rampant in New York in those days. I was always amazed that they completely accepted Harold and his super-minstrel-show antics. They loved it—and adored him.[7]

Some of the songs Arlen and Koehler wrote for the club in 1932 (starting with that year, the shows were called <u>Cotton Club</u>

Harold Arlen. (Museum of the City of New York)

Parades) reflect their ability to produce material expressive of local cultural traits, both attractive ("Harlem Holiday") and unattractive ("The Wail of the Reefer Man"). They also faithfully reproduced black genre songs, such as the blue blues for which Bessie Smith and Ethel Waters were noted. Leitha Hill was the torch singer in residence at the club at that time, and for her, Arlen and Koehler produced such songs as "Pool Room Papa," "My Military Man" and "High Flyin' Man." None of these songs bears Arlen's name. They were the sort of shocking songs that could be found only on "race records," and as such, Arlen felt they were a bit too "specialized."

The song Arlen and Koehler wrote for the club in 1932 that became a national hit was "I've Got the World on a String," which Aida Ward sang in the show. Other numbers included "In the Silence of the Night," "That's What I Hate About Love" and "New Kind of Rhythm." And for Cab Calloway, and the Cotton Club audience, a return of that favorite club personality in "Minnie the Moocher's Wedding Day."

Owney Madden usually showed up on opening nights, or a few nights after an opening, but he was not around for the fall 1932 show. In July he had voluntarily re-entered Sing Sing. Ostensibly the action was taken because of a parole violation, but since only a minor technicality was in question, Madden clearly wanted to be back in prison. Although his exact reasons are not known, it is likely that he was tired of being a mob leader and wanted to retire. Returning to prison may have been a way of "clearing up" his 1916 sentence. Also, he may have felt that being in prison, he would be treated more leniently by the Internal Revenue Service. In May of 1933, from prison, he requested an easement on his income taxes for 1931, in which there was an alleged deficiency of $20,493. He'd been having trouble with the IRS since 1924, yet between that year and 1931, claims on him by the government had totaled only $70,000. As Madden had accumulated considerable wealth through his various rackets, it is certain that he had a very clever tax lawyer in Joseph Shalleek. The theory that Madden re-entered Sing Sing primarily in order to clear up loose ends in his relationship both with the courts and with the IRS is supported by the fact that upon his release from prison later in 1933, he went into retirement in Hot Springs, Arkansas.

Chapter 5

PROHIBITION IS REPEALED AND THE DEPRESSION DEEPENS

In January 1933 the proposed constitutional amendment for repeal of Prohibition went to the states for ratification, and apparently confirmation was so certain that the next month beer returned legally, a "foretaste," as one writer put it, of things to come.

Repeal was greeted with mixed feelings in New York. Obtaining bootleg liquor, no matter how easily it could be done, did involve a bit of daring and bravado, and the partying crowd bemoaned legitimization. Syndicates like Owney Madden's now faced government crackdowns of far greater strength than during the period of Prohibition, and those who had opened clubs as outlets for their bootleg products feared that the combination of Depression and repeal would be extremely bad for business. That fear proved real for a number of Harlem night spots, which closed that year. Connie's Inn, one of the Harlem "Big Three," left Harlem to the remaining "Big Two" and moved to greener pastures downtown.

Opposite: Bessie Dudley. (Lincoln Center Library)

"The Spectre That Must Be Laid." Drawing by Rollin Kirby. (Museum of the City of New York)

By 1933 the effects of the Depression had taken their toll upon the mood as well as the pocketbook of the country. As average annual per capita income tumbled from $681 in 1929 to $495 in 1933, the optimistic view that the Depression would be over almost as soon as it began had been replaced by a more realistic attitude. The popular song of 1932 was "Brother, Can You Spare a Dime?" While the regular clientele of the Cotton Club seems not to have been seriously affected by the effects of the stock-market crash, and while the entertainers seemed as gay as ever, they could hardly miss the long free-soup lines, the beggars on the corners, the gloom that descended over the streets of Harlem. The performers began to discuss openly the ironic contrast between the places where they lived and the place where they worked. Accordingly, the Cotton Club became civic-minded.

In December 1932, the club began passing out Christmas baskets to the needy. The gesture received wide publicity, for the management always made sure that at least one of its top stars helped in doling out the baskets. New York's social consciousness, in the institutional sense, did not develop until later, and for a while the Cotton Club conducted the largest free kitchen in Harlem.

In the late winter of 1933, business was booming at the club, partly due to an influx of former patrons of the Harlem Connie's Inn, and the management could look forward to even higher receipts in the spring, for after two years of recording stints and playing to sellout audiences as the Cotton Club Band, Duke Ellington and his orchestra were returning in March and would be at the club for the spring show, set to open April 6th. The club's management could count on the success of that show, for Ellington and company would ensure it, but they had no way of foreseeing what a sensation Ethel Waters would be.

When Ethel Waters had arrived back in New York in 1930, after playing one-night stands in a variety of cities, Herman Stark had staged an "Ethel Waters Night." This had endeared the club to her. She was not yet a star, although she was fairly well known on the entertainment circuit. She had that indefinable "something" that everyone in show business talks about but no one ever tries to explain, and she had possessed that quality from the very beginning.

Ethel Waters had begun her career in New York some years prior to 1930 at Edmond's, on Fifth Avenue and 130th Street. It was a basement dive, patronized by pimps, hookers and gamblers and given to "pansy" fashion parades. Waters later described it as "the last stop on the way down." Most entertainers, particularly

singers, had a hard time at Edmond's. They exhausted themselves trying to be heard above the inattentive din of conversation. Often they simply stopped trying. Not Ethel, as she was simply known. The tall brown-skinned girl had presence. When it came time for her number she would stride to the center of the floor, strike a nonchalant and half-contemptuous pose, and wait. Soon all became silent, and they would remain silent and attentive as she sang the blues, infusing it with her own particular style, bringing to reality its potential for tragedy

and heartbreak. There was no doubt that Ethel was an original, and it was not long before she left Edmond's to go on to better things.

By early 1933, when she returned to New York once again, Ethel Waters' personal life was at an ebb. She and her second husband, Eddie Matthews, had just broken up. Her career, too, was at a standstill. She'd been playing stints in Chicago and Cicero—Al Capone territory. In fact, the club at which she had sung in Cicero was one of Capone's. Working in Capone-con-

Street scene—Peace Shine—3¢. Fifth Avenue between 133 and 134 streets.
Photo by Grossman, 1939. (Museum of the City of New York)

Prohibition Is Repealed and the Depression Deepens

Above: Ethel Waters. (Museum of the City of New York)
Below: Harold Arlen, Morton Da Costa, Robert Fryer and Carol Lawrence. (Culver Pictures)

Opposite: Ethel Waters. (Culver Pictures)

trolled clubs tended to "mark" performers, and to make other club owners wary of hiring them. Also, such work was rather nerve-racking. As Ethel Waters would later say, ". . . though I'm a child of the underworld I must say that I prefer working for people who never laid eyes on an Italian pineapple or a sawed-off shotgun. I went back to New York glad to be alive."[1]

For Herman Stark, Ethel Waters' return to New York seemed like the proverbial perfect timing. Arlen and Koehler had written a potentially exciting number for the new Cotton Club show, for which the Ellington band had created special storm effects. Ethel was just the woman to give it the rendition it deserved. It was a torch song, and Ethel had a solid reputation for doing such numbers in her own, very personal way.

Ethel was pleased that Stark wanted her, but even though she sorely needed exposure in a club whose underworld backing was at least less conspicuous than that of the club in which she had been working in Illinois, she was sure of her talent and appeal. She was not one to "sell herself cheap." She asked for the highest salary Stark had ever paid a star.

For his part, Stark knew he needed a particular type of performer and a particular type of voice, and he was a sufficiently good businessman to be willing to pay for what he wanted.

The song about which everyone at the Cotton Club was so excited had been created in such an offhand manner that few could have foreseen the impact it would have. Arlen had been thinking of Cab Calloway when he wrote it, but the lyrics Ted Koehler had written for the tune were not Calloway lyrics. In radical departure from his usual style, Koehler only listened to the tune a few times before he

Best Wishes
to Joe
Sincerely
Ethel Waters

Ethel Waters, when she was in the Cotton Club's Revue in Harlem. (Museum of the City of New York)

had the words. Altogether the creative process for the song took about thirty minutes, after which the two went out to get a sandwich. Running through it again later, Arlen and Koehler began to hear in the song more than what they had so casually wrought, and when they rehearsed it at the club the response was more excited than it had been to any of their earlier hits; this was A SONG!

Ethel listened to the number and agreed that it was indeed wonderful. But she felt that the piece should express more human emotion and not rely upon complex sound effects. She asked to take the lead sheet home and work on it.

When she returned, Ethel made a stipulation. She had worked on the song and knew she could infuse it with the emotion she felt it deserved, but she wished to sing it only at one show a night. The song was "Stormy Weather."

The success of Ethel and "Stormy Weather" tended to obscure the rest of this, the twenty-second of the Cotton Club shows, which was a masterpiece of its kind, featuring eighteen scenes in addition to the Ellington orchestra's overture, finale and interim tunes. The first scene was entitled "Harlem Hospital," a typical vaudeville skit with a sensual twist featuring Sally Goodings as Head Nurse, Dusty Fletcher as Dr. Jones, Cora LaRedd as Doctor's Assistant and George Dewey Washington (who was also appearing in the Broadway production of Strike Me Pink, starring Jimmy Durante), as Mr. Cotton Club.

In the second scene Washington reappeared to sing "Calico Days." The song "Happy As the Day Is Long" was used in the skit titled "Harlem Spirit," as was the song "Raisin' the Rent." Cora LaRedd and

Ethel Waters and chorus. (Collection of Duncan Schiedt)

Henry "Rubber Legs" Williams did their specialty dances, and Sally Goodings sang the expected adult number, "I'm Lookin' for Another Handy Man."

But then came the eleventh scene, and it managed to eclipse all that had gone before and all that would come after. It was titled "Cabin in the Cotton Club" and the set was uncommonly simple—a log-cabin backdrop and a single lamppost. As the scene opened, Ethel Waters leaned against the lamppost, a lone deep-blue spotlight on her. After she sang "Stormy Weather" alone, the scene faded softly into the next, in which George Dewey Washington and the choir sang responses to her choruses. With the help of special lighting effects, the female dancers were blended into the tableau to dance to the tune of the song. The entire production was so effectively presented, so movingly performed that the audience, at first silenced, filled the room with a thunderous applause as they recovered. On opening night there were at least a dozen encores.

Other scenes followed—dances, skits, specialty acts, and then, the grand finale. It was a long show, but it moved well; the costumes were lavish, the scenery perfect, the talent marvelous. But it was the eleventh scene that people talked about, and came especially to see.

Years later Ethel Waters explained: " 'Stormy Weather' was the perfect expression of my mood, and I found release in singing it each evening. When I got out there in the middle of the Cotton Club floor, I was telling things I couldn't frame in words. I was singing the story of my misery and confusion, of the misunderstandings in my life I couldn't straighten out, the story of wrongs and outrages done to me by people I had loved and trusted."[2] "If there's anything I owe Eddie Matthews," she would sometimes comment ruefully, "it's that he enabled me to do one hell of a job on the song 'Stormy Weather.' "

The "Stormy Weather Show," as it came to be called, was one of the most successful ever staged at the Cotton Club. Within

Opposite: Cab Calloway and Bill Robinson.
(Culver Pictures)

a few days the song and the singer were the talk of New York, the message carried by the newspaper columnists as well as by word of mouth, specifically by such people as: Jimmy Durante, Milton Berle, Lillian Roth, Eleanor Holm, Lew Diamond, Steve Trilling, George Raft (who had "made it" by then), Fannie Ward, Eddie Duchin, Ray Bolger, Wilma Cox, Ruby Bloom, Mary Lou Dix and Bert Lahr.

People who rarely made the night club scene did so now. People who had never before visited the Cotton Club came to see the show. Irving Berlin did not often visit New York's spots, but he had heard about Ethel Waters and "Stormy Weather," and he traveled to Harlem to hear her sing. Berlin was writing the music for a new revue that Sam H. Harris was producing and he wanted to inject a serious note into it. After hearing Ethel Waters at the Cotton Club, Berlin knew that she was the one to do it.

Rehearsals for Berlin's revue began two weeks after Ethel closed at the Cotton Club. As Thousands Cheer was a hit on Broadway, and Ethel Waters' career took off. She would always credit "Stormy Weather" as the turning point in her career. Later she would have occasion to thank Arlen again, for writing "Happiness Is Just a Thing Called Joe."

Within a few weeks after the show's opening, "Stormy Weather" was selling fantastically well on records and sheet music, and it occurred to a young advertiser/promoter named Robert Wachsman that a vaudeville act could be built around the song. He visited Arlen and persuaded him to audition at Radio City Music Hall, where he was offered a ten-to-twelve-week contract. All he needed was the club's permission to use the song.

When Wachsman approached him a few days later, Stark reacted negatively. "Stormy Weather" was still current in the club's show, and Stark felt that using the song simultaneously in vaudeville would hurt the show. However, he left the final decision up to Big Frenchy DeMange. That night Wachsman returned to the club with Arlen, but Big Frenchy was nowhere to be found. They waited all night, and finally, around seven, he appeared for breakfast. Taking a deep breath, Wachsman launched into the most fast-talking and persuasive argument he could muster. Far from hurting the Cotton Club show, he insisted, using "Stormy Weather" at Radio City would attract patrons to the club. Big Frenchy did not appear to pay much attention to Wachsman, and when the promoter finished speaking, he was greeted with silence. "Well," Wachsman asked in frustration, "What do you think?"

"I t'ink it's de nuts," said Big Frenchy, "Where's my ham an' eggs?"[3]

Permission was granted, and the "Stormy Weather" act opened at Radio City. However, it is likely that it would have been staged even without the club's permission, for Radio City had arranged for the purchase of a special wind machine even before Arlen auditioned for the management of the Music Hall.

Each year there was a substantial turnover within the Cotton Club cast. Featured performers, naturally, did only one show, or at the most two. The chorus dancers and singers generally stayed for at least a year, and some for several. However, after the closing of each show, a few performers always left. Turnover was particularly high among the Cotton Club Girls, some of whom, like Isabel Washington, left to pursue major show-business careers of

their own. Others never gained great renown, but if they had played even one season at the club, the billing "Formerly of the Cotton Club" earned them bookings at theaters and lesser clubs. Still others, and perhaps most who left, did so to get married. After the closing of the second Cotton Club Parade, the "Stormy Weather Show," there were several places in the chorus line to be filled.

Lena Horne auditioned for one of them. Lena was from Brooklyn, by way of the Bronx and the South, and she was barely sixteen years old. During the height of the Depression, her mother, who was "of good family," and her stepfather were unable to earn enough money to support the family. Partly in economic desperation, and partly

because she herself had tried and failed in show business, Lena's mother decided to try to get Lena into the Cotton Club chorus line. She had known Elida Webb, dance mistress at the club, for years.

Elida Webb and Lena Horne's mother had tried to break into show business at the same time, and while Mrs. Horne had not made it, Miss Webb had—as a choreographer. As a dancer, she had been a member of the chorus line in Shuffle Along, had discovered dancer Fredi Washington, and claimed to have invented the Charleston. Her claim is hard to dispute, for she was among the most talented dancers in New York. Her experience with Fredi Washington had led her into choreography, and she had been with the Cotton Club for a number of years, among the first blacks to break the "whites only" barrier that surrounded the creative aspects of the Cotton Club shows. Elida Webb saw potential

There was integration to a certain extent. We were there; the performers could go. Even if whites come to see blacks perform, you still have integration. If you had to depend solely on the attendance of a Negro audience, one hundred per-cent, you'd never make it. I think that we were doing something that had to be done, when we were performing, when we were making it possible for the people to come see us.

The Cotton Club wasn't a segregated club, it was a club where you had to be somebody to get in there.

—Cab Calloway

in Lena Horne, and she was willing to do everything she could for the daughter of an old friend.

Because of Elida Webb, Lena Horne was able to avoid much of the red tape with which girls auditioning at the club were usually confronted. Still, Lena could not have felt she had much of an edge when she and her mother arrived for the audition.

The tryouts took place during the rehearsal period for the new show, the one that was to follow the ''Stormy Weather Show,'' with Cab Calloway's orchestra and with Aida Ward as the star.

Herman Stark was auditioning some new specialty numbers as well as girls for the chorus. It was morning, and the glamour of the Cotton Club, which Lena had imagined while listening to radio broadcasts from the club, was nowhere to be seen in the dark and cavernous ballroom. The air was heavy with stale cigarette smoke, and one had to grope through a jungle of chairs upended on tables. In the center of the dance floor a work lamp cast eerie shadows over the bodies seated or standing in a semicircle around the arc of the lamp's spill. Periodically a name was called out and a girl advanced to the center of the spotlight. At a signal the pianist began to play a fast number, and the girl launched into a routine of her swiftest and most intricate steps. Then, ''That's enough!'' and the pianist would accompany the girl as she sang a few bars. With that, the audition was over.

Lena Horne's heart sank as she watched the other auditioners. They seemed so talented, so self-assured. All were older than she, although a girl sitting near her, and with whom she nervously whispered while the other auditions were going on, was just slightly older.

''I could carry a tune, but I could hardly have been called a singer,'' Lena Horne

later recalled. ''I could dance a little, but I could hardly be called a dancer, I was tall and skinny and I had very little going for me except a pretty face and long, long hair that framed it rather nicely. Also, I was young—about sixteen—and despite the sundry vicissitudes of my life, very, very innocent. As it turned out, this was all that was needed.''[4]

When she heard the call ''Horne? Lena Horne? She here?'' Lena became terrified. She advanced to the tiny lighted spot. She could hear the others' voices but could not see their faces. She stared into the darkness. The piano began to play, but she couldn't move. Somehow, above the other voices and the music, she heard her mother's voice urging her on. She started to whirl, and she spun faster and faster. When the music stopped, she did not. Her wild steps continued until Elida Webb grabbed her arm and forced her to halt. Everyone in the place was roaring with sheer glee.

Lena and Winnie Johnson, the girl who had become her friend while she waited for her audition, were the only two hired that day. She would receive a salary of $25 a week (salesclerks were earning between $5 and $10 weekly; top-notch New York stenographers, $16) to do three shows a night, seven days a week. She had to dodge the truant officer (she was supposed to be attending Girls' High School in Brooklyn), and she felt very young and naïve compared to the worldly older girls in the chorus. Her mother's friends were horrified that Lena was working in a club run by gangsters, where liquor was sold openly despite Prohibition, and where the chorus girls were rumored to be hired for purposes other than dancing. Lena, however, experienced very few threats to her innocence.

To Prince Johnson
with
sincere best wishes
—Leana
/36

Her very youth protected her. "I was jail bait and no one ever made a pass at me or suggested I go out with one of the customers, which happened all the time to the older girls. The owners apparently figured that any kind of fooling around with underage girls was the quickest way to lose their license."[5]

Her father and his friends also represented a protective force. Her father was a real "sporting man," which was one reason why her mother had divorced him. His friends were the gamblers, the numbers people, the men who had the binocular concessions at the track. They were among the few blacks admitted into the club, although they were always given side booths, near the kitchen. They had known Lena since she was a baby, and they formed a sort of underground protective association.

Then, too, her mother was a conscientious chaperone. She accompanied Lena to the club nearly every night and sat in the dressing room until her daughter was ready to go home. She lectured Lena constantly about being a "good" girl. In fact, she created such a special aura around her daughter that the other girls concluded that Lena thought herself better than they. She was an outsider, prevented by her youth and her mother from being "one of the gang," and she was very aware of that. Thus, it meant a great deal to her when Cab Calloway remembered her.

A few weeks before Calloway's band arrived at the Cotton Club, it had been featured at a charity affair at the Paramount in Brooklyn. Some of the Brooklyn Junior Debs, of which Lena was a member, had served as hostesses. On Lena's first day at the Cotton Club, she was resting on the dance floor during a rehearsal rest period when Calloway strolled by. He caught sight of Lena, hesitated a moment, then called out, "Good Gawd Amighty, there's Brooklyn!" He walked over to her and introduced her to the musician with him. From then on, he was her hero, and she waited eagerly every day for his "Hiya, Brooklyn!"

The first show Lena was in was not one of the Cotton Club's big hit shows. Arlen and Koehler did not write the songs for it; they

Let us turn now to the gentle subject of hooch. Harlem is hooch-ridden. He is a bold man who will undertake to say what part of a city like New York, with its many congested foreign and native quarters, is the wettest. The wash of the booze sea has not left Harlem out; that district may well claim a deeper inundation than any other.

—Winthrop D. Lane, "Ambushed in the City: The Grim Side of Harlem"

were busy in Hollywood working on the score for <u>Let's Fall in Love</u>, their first film assignment. Among the songwriters who contributed to the Cotton Club's twenty-third show were Jimmy Van Heusen and Harold Arlen's younger brother, Jerry, who collaborated on the song "There's a House in Harlem for Sale."

As usual, a major part of the show was built around the latest dance craze. At that time the craze was the fan dance, which Sally Rand had made famous. The chorus girls carried huge fans, and if they were not quite as naked as Miss Rand was, they were close to it. Lena Horne's costume consisted of exactly three feathers. "I sensed that the white people in the audience saw nothing but my flesh, and its color, onstage," she later remarked.

Lena had begun to take singing lessons shortly after coming to the Cotton Club, and her mother reminded the club's managers at every opportunity that her little girl could sing as well as dance. She enlisted the help of Cab Calloway, and Flournoy Miller, in boosting Lena. Miller had been in on the production of <u>Shuffle Along</u> with Sissle and Blake and had been partly responsible for discovering Florence Mills, Josephine Baker, Gertrude Saunders, and a number of others who had started in <u>Shuffle Along</u> and become stars. He had been hired by the Cotton Club as part of the comedy team of Miller and Mantan, and while the Cotton Club management expected him to be a comedian rather than a producer, they did occasionally ask his advice and they respected his opinions. With Cab Calloway, Flournoy Miller and her

mother for cheerleaders, Lena was bound to be given a chance.

One night that chance came. Aida Ward developed a sore throat and had to stay home, and Lena was told to fill in. Calloway gave her a quick rehearsal—she'd heard the number so often she knew the lyrics by heart—and she sang the number in all three shows. The audience was most appreciative, as Stark had expected they would be. Lena's voice wasn't anything special, as the older chorus girls did not hesitate to point out to her, but she was young, innocent and beautiful. Her body was not yet fully developed, but it was lithe and graceful, and she had a dazzling smile and immensely expressive eyes and hands.

The next night Aida Ward came back, and that was the end of Lena's feature-dom.

Lena continued to dream, and to study intently the styles of successful singers. After hours in the dressing room she would entertain the other girls with her impressions. One of her best was of Ethel Waters singing "Stormy Weather." Ethel still appeared at the Cotton Club from time to time, and the story goes that one night in her own dressing room she heard Lena imitating her. She walked into the chorus girls' dressing room, much to Lena's embarrassment. "It was just in fun, Miss Waters," she is supposed to have mumbled.

"In fun, girl?" Ethel cried. "That's fine singing. You get busy and don't let anybody stop you from singing from now on."

Years later, when the picture <u>Stormy Weather</u> was made, Lena Horne was the star.

Chapter 6

Prohibition repeal was ratified by the required number of states and became official in December 1933—a Christmas present from America to itself. The Cotton Club was not pleased with the gift. The deepening Depression with its accompanying high prices had cut into the club's profits, and the end of Prohibition took some of the excitement out of New York night life in general. Ordinarily Stark, DeMange and company could count on the excellence of the shows to keep the crowds coming, but the spring 1934 show was one they could not count on. Of all shows, this had to be the one with a brand-new and untested Cotton Club band. Cab Calloway's orchestra had left the club at the close of the fall 1933 show and Jimmie Lunceford's band was hired as a replacement in January 1934. The Cotton Club management was highly dubious about the situation.

The club's managers were not particularly musically inclined. They knew only what their customers liked. The patrons had

Opposite: Josephine Baker. (Culver Pictures)

liked Duke Ellington's band with its jungle rhythms. They had liked Cab Calloway's personality. To the uninitiated, both played "Negro music." The music of Jimmie Lunceford's band was a different sound altogether.

After receiving his B.A. in music at Fisk University and doing graduate work at Fisk and New York's City College, Lunceford had taken a job teaching music at Manassa High School in Memphis, Tennessee. The Lunceford band was organized with students in his class. When they graduated and went to Fisk University, he went with them, taking a job as an assistant professor of music. By the time the students graduated from Fisk, the band was known throughout the South, and Lunceford

decided to take them to New York. By that time a few outsiders had joined the band, but the core of the group was Lunceford's students, and Lunceford was still their teacher, always emphasizing discipline and musicianship.

Lunceford was no showman. In fact, he was a very restrained personality. But he was an exquisite professional, and this quality appealed to the public as much as the showmanship of a Cab Calloway, although at the time it came to the Cotton Club the band was just beginning to acquire a reputation.

Nearly as important to the band as Lunceford himself was the first trumpet player, Sy Oliver. He was the band's arranger, and

Andrew Preer's Cotton Club orchestra, 1924.

he created a higly distinctive sound, a fuller sound with a fuller ensemble than many other arrangers used. Rather than the slow dance tempos or fast, show tempos of other bands, he preferred a medium tempo, with an exciting bounce. Some of the band's most successful recordings, like "Organ Grinder Swing" and "'T'aint What You Do," were Oliver arrangements.

Arlen and Koehler returned to the club for its spring 1934 show, the first show at the club for Lunceford and his orchestra. Accordingly, perhaps, this show was much more successful than the fall 1933 show, and it ran for some eight months. It starred Adelaide Hall, and one of her feature numbers, "Primitive Prima Donna," became one of the most popular Cotton Club songs. More famous was the song "Ill Wind," which she also sang in the show. Intended to be a sequel to "Stormy Weather," and just as show-stopping, it failed to meet such expectations. Nevertheless, it proved to be one of Arlen and Koehler's best.

The Cotton Club Boys were introduced in this show. The Cotton Club Girls had become an institution in their own right, and the club's management, feeling they needed a new gimmick, decided to use a line of young male dancers. Dozens were auditioned, ten were chosen: Howard "Stretch" Johnson, Charles "Chink" Collins,

Jimmie Lunceford orchestra. Cotton Club, 1934. (Collection of Duncan Schiedt)

William Smith, Walter Shepherd, Tommy Porter, Maxie Armstrong, Louis Brown, Jimmy Wright, Thomas "Chink" Lee and Eddie Morton. They were made a feature act of the show and their new style of group dancing, in which all moved together in rhythmic unison, was immediately popular. Soon other groups were attempting to imitate their precision style, but no one then could successfully duplicate it. At the end of the eight-month run they had become an established feature of the club. "We knew from the way the folks received us that we were going to be around for a long time," one of the boys later recalled. Juano Hernandez danced in his exotic, quivering style in an exciting voodoo scene, and there were lively chorus routines in addition to other featured numbers. All in all, the show was a typical, fast-paced Dan Healy production, and with Arlen and Koehler back, it was bound to be a success.

This 1934 Cotton Club Parade proved to be a compendium of gambles, for it was also the first show for dancer Avon Long. Like the Lunceford band, Long was hired by the club's management despite certain misgivings. Always before, the club's featured male dancers had been of the "eccentric" type, like Earl "Snakehips" Tucker and Jigsaw Jackson, contortionistic and exhibitionistic. Avon Long's style, while it had a distinctive jazz beat, was subtle, gliding and smooth. Yet he was strikingly individualistic, and the management had decided to take a chance. Anyway, he had an excellent voice. He was to do the Arlen-Koehler song "As Long As I Live" with a female partner.

The show was Lena Horne's second at the club, and as the opening drew nearer, she and her mother were resigned to the fact that she would get no break there. The show was cast, and she would be in the chorus, as usual.

Then, at practically the last minute, the girl who was to be Long's partner quit, and Lena was given her first big break. She became a featured performer at the Cotton Club after less than a year, and like all other featured Cotton Club performers, this meant a great deal of exposure for her. Columnist Louis Sobol reported about an evening in March 1934: "I find that among the folks who were present that evening were Irving and Ellin Berlin, and with them film producer Samuel Goldwyn and his wife; playwright Sam Behrman, Gregory Ratoff, Paul Whiteman and Margaret Livingstone; producer George White; man-about-town Jules Glaenzer; harmonica maestro Borrah Minevitch; Cobina Wright; Marilyn Miller, Lillian Roth, Lee Shubert, Miriam Hopkins, Jo Frisco, Ted Husing and Eddie Duchin."[1] If just one of these people noticed her, Lena could be on her way to a major career.

Before the show ended its run, Lena had a job on Broadway in a show called Dance with Your Gods, starring Rex Ingraham and Georgette Harvey. Lena's was a bit part; she played A Quadroon Girl, but it was Broadway nevertheless. Once Lena learned what the producer of the show had been forced to go through in order to get her, she prized the opportunity even more.

The producer, Lawrence Schwab, had to persuade the head of the Broadway mob to intercede with Madden's people to convince them to agree to Lena's performing in the show. An arrangement was made whereby she was allowed to skip the first performance at the Cotton Club, but she was expected to rush uptown and work the late shows. All the trouble was practically for nothing. Gods closed after about two weeks, ending Lena Horne's debut on Broadway.

During her first show at the Cotton Club,

there was just one, the female performers were discouraged from using it and told that it was for the patrons. She suddenly saw the inadequate backstage facilities and the conditions of the girls' dressing room:

I saw that twenty-five of us were herded into one tiny, crowded, windowless dressing room in which we had barely space enough to sit before our make-up mirror. I saw that it was littered with loaded ashtrays, coffee containers, newspapers, make-up, fan magazines, the half-eaten sandwiches and cartons of chop suey we were too tired to gulp down, and the bags in which some of the girls brought their knitting or mending. I realized that it reeked of perfume and cigarette smoke, stale perspiration, and the mingled odors of our many meals. And I longed for a breath of fresh air and some place I could stretch my aching limbs and go to sleep.[2]

But she was grateful for the job. She was also aware that if the other club employees—the waiters and busboys and cooks and kitchen helpers and clean-up squad—were not working at the Cotton Club, they probably wouldn't be working at all. Nevertheless, Lena began to feel exploited. Her $25-a-week salary, which seemed so ample at first, proved to be just barely sufficient to support her family. Times were hard and prices were high, and without the money she brought in each week, she had no idea how they would have managed. Even the truant officer realized this, and while he still visited Mrs. Horne once a week, as was his duty, he took to writing down "missing" in his report on Lena.

Sometimes Lena did not take home $25 a week. Under the contract her mother had signed, and under which all the girls worked, her pay could be docked for lateness, missing a rehearsal, and a long list of minor infractions. The girls received no fringe benefits, such as meals. The club was

Lena had been awestruck by the club, by the wealth of its patrons, by the notoriety of its owners. For the first few weeks of her second show, she was excited about her feature number with Avon Long and bewildered by the rapid pace of her career. But after Gods closed, and she settled into the routine of the spring 1934 show, she began to see the club in a more realistic light. Things she had hardly noticed or thought about before became uncomfortably evident to her. Previously she had been so fascinated by the older chorus girls—listening to their gossip, admiring their sophisticated clothes, envying the frequent male telephone calls they received—that she had failed to notice the conditions in which they worked. Now she began to question why there was only one ladies' room in the club, and why, given that

renowned for its food, especially the Mexican and Chinese dishes and the Southern fried chicken, and although there was a great deal of waste, as there is in most restaurant kitchens, the girls couldn't even get leftovers. Only under one circumstance were they given a meal at the club, and that was when the entire show was taken upstate to entertain the prisoners at Sing Sing. Lena, who was constantly hungry in those days, remembers those trips with fondness.

Among the performers there was considerable resentment against the Cotton Club management, and Lena began to pay closer attention to the older girls' gripe sessions, understanding their feelings better now. The chief source of discontent was money. They were sure the club was making a fortune and they felt that their hard work helped bring about this monetary success. They resented having their pay docked for petty reasons and not getting paid extra for the additional performances

and benefits they did. But when Lena asked why some of the older girls did not tell the management how they felt, they assured her it would do no good. They would simply be told to "take it or leave it" and that they could easily be replaced. Also, the "boys" were not above using muscle to keep truculent performers in line, and that went for their relatives as well. Lena's mother and stepfather were impatient for her to have a spot in the shows as a singer. One night after hours her stepfather went to see the club bosses to try to persuade them in a forceful manner—a mistake, as he would soon learn. Some of the bosses' hoods followed him out into the street and beat him severely.

The general attitude among the Cotton Club veterans was one of resignation and determination to stick it out for the time being and hope something better would come along.

The Cotton Club performers also resented the strict division between white

These places . . . are no longer mine but theirs. Not that I'm barred, any more than they were 7 or 8 years ago. Once known, I'm even welcomed, just as some of them used to be. But the complexion of the place is theirs not mine . . .

As another observer has put it to me since, time was when white people went to Negro cabarets to see how Negroes acted; now Negroes go to these same cabarets to see how white people act.

—Rudolph Fisher, "The Caucasian Storms Harlem"

and black in the creation, production and realization of the shows. Occasionally Duke Ellington did the music for a score, or a black arranger was called in to do a special number. Clarence Robinson, stage director at the theater in Philadelphia where Ellington's band had been playing before its first stint at the Cotton Club, was one of the best in his field. Occasionally he was called in to work with the show. But these were exceptions to the rule. In general, whites controlled every creative or lucrative phase of the show, from music score and lyrics, to staging, to choreographing, to costume and set design. The blacks . . . well, they performed. As Lena Horne put it:

The Cotton Club veterans felt they were blocked and used by white people. They were full of stories about how white people had drawn on their experience, taken their ideas for individual numbers—even for complete shows—and given them nothing in return. Not even a credit line in a program, much less any payment . . .

They'd talk resentfully about how the town was filled with gifted, creative people. There were lyric writers like Andy Razaf, W. C. Handy, Maceo Pinkard, Eubie Blake. There were dance directors like Leonard Harper, Charlie Davis. And right in the company itself, there was Flournoy Miller, college graduate, who'd been one of the talented four—Miller, Lyles, Sissle & Blake—who'd written, directed, cast, produced, and appeared in that sensation of the twenties—"Shuffle Along." . . . They had hired him as a comedian in the team of Miller & Mantan, and that was the limit of his actual work.[3]

Lena did not feel the same resentment. She was young and optimistic, and she had not been exposed to many of the more disagreeable aspects of racial or show business politics. She disliked being hungry, and she wanted more money, and she felt the club was unfair in docking her

pay for minor infractions, but she did not become bitterly resentful until the night her stepfather and some of his friends were denied entrance to the club.

She would have to quit the club immediately, but her mother realized it would be foolish to leave with no prospect of another job. Angry about the incident, too, she settled for requesting a raise in Lena's salary. She got $5 more a week. Then she went to Flournoy Miller and asked him to help Lena once again, this time to get her out of the Cotton Club. A short while later an audition for Lena was arranged before Noble Sissle, who was then touring with his highly successful orchestra. She did not have to dance, for obviously she was a good dancer if she was at the Cotton Club. She sang just one song, "Dinner for One, Please James," and was hired.

Quitting the Cotton Club was not easy. Not only would she leave a hole in the chorus line, but also Avon Long would be without a partner for the "As Long As I Live" number. The attitude of the Cotton Club bosses was that they could fire anyone they wanted, but no one was supposed to quit. On Lena's last night at the club, both her mother and stepfather confronted the club bosses, who were furious. When verbal persuasion and threats did not work, they beat up her stepfather, pushed his head down a toilet bowl and then threw him out.

Lena and her mother wanted to leave, but one of the boys was sent backstage to make sure Lena did her shows. Thus, while her frightened mother was wringing her hands in the dressing room, a terror-stricken Lena went through the movements of three interminably long shows as if in a nightmare. After the final show ended they left

Above: Jimmie Lunceford, 1940. (Culver Pictures)
Below: Lunceford brass section. (Culver Pictures)

the club under the protection of a crowd of chorus girls, never to see it again. Quite literally, the three Hornes ran away with Noble Sissle's orchestra.

Lena Horne was not the only one to leave the Cotton Club after the spring 1934 show, although her departure was certainly the most dramatic. Harold Arlen left, too, terminating not only his relationship with the club but also, at least for some years, his successful partnership with Ted Koehler.

During rehearsals Arlen had been offered the chance to do the music for a full-scale revue to be produced by the Shuberts. While he wanted very much to accept the offer, Arlen was deeply troubled about having to leave Koehler and their warm and productive relationship. What worried him most was how to tell his friend. At last, unable to do so orally, he wrote a note and gave it to Koehler one day at rehearsal. When the rehearsal was over, Koehler read the note, and his reaction was typical in its straightforwardness: Arlen would be a fool not to accept the offer. That night Arlen went out and got drunk.

Arlen would look back on those years at the club with mostly positive feelings. Other than having had to write some songs he considered in bad taste, the only really disagreeable memory was the time when he needed an operation and the Cotton Club heads would not give him the advance on his salary needed to pay for it. Ted Koehler stayed on at the club to do lyrics for a few more shows before moving on. Years later he and Arlen collaborated again.

The Cotton Club still had successful shows after Arlen's departure. In fact, the very next show, in the spring of 1935, was a considerable success. The Cotton Club Boys, who'd proved so popular in the previous

show, were brought back, although seven of the original ten were gone. One, Roy Carter, had died late in 1934, and the others had gone on to various things, not all fruitful. They were a hard-working, fast-living, heavy-drinking group of young men, who spent their money on smart clothes and pretty women, and they were not particularly responsible employees. The newcomers to the group, which consisted of only seven members for the spring 1935 show, were Al Alstock, Ernest Frazier, Freddie Heron and Jules Adger.

The Lunceford band also returned, for the misgivings of the club's management had proved groundless. The club's patrons liked his style, and so did a lot of other musicians. By the middle of 1935 the Amsterdam News, Harlem's weekly newspaper, was commenting: "Lunceford-Lunceford-Lunceford. That's all you hear in Harlem now."

The show came to be called the "Truckin' Show," after the dance and song of that name, and the title was apt for the times. "Truckin' " meant carrying on despite setbacks. "Keep on truckin' "—it suggested a laborious uphill climb along hard roads, and it symbolized, for many, life itself in the mid-thirities. While almost no one was unaffected, there were certain people and certain areas that seemed to carry more of their share of the burden. One of those areas was Harlem.

Jimmie Lunceford orchestra. (Collection of Duncan Schiedt)

End of an Era

As the Depression deepened, violence in Harlem increased dramatically. Caught in the economic squeeze, the various mobs, which had coexisted in relative peace during Prohibition, began to fight among themselves. The "Mad Dog" situation in 1931–1932 was a tame foretaste compared to what came later. While downtown revelers who came uptown were not targets of the mob violence, quite frequently they became unwillingly involved in it. As reports of injury and death to innocent bystanders caught in the path of stray bullets increased, attendance at the white-oriented Harlem clubs began to decrease.

If anyone was having a hard time "truckin' " in the mid-thirties, it was the residents of Harlem. By 1934, according to the Urban League, 80 percent of them were on relief. They felt trapped. The pride of the early twenties had given way to a new militancy, and a strong anti-white resentment. A young Reverend Adam Clayton Powell, Jr., who would shortly begin to lead boycotts of stores and buses and public utility companies to force hiring of blacks, identified and verbalized the sources of that resentment in a column in the Amsterdam News. Each week the column "Soap Box" dealt with a particular area in which blacks were discriminated against or exploited or used. One piece, entitled "Sharecroppers," addressed itself to the exploitation of black performers, particularly black orchestras, by their white managers:

The truth of it is that they are only sharecropping. Duke Ellington is just a musical sharecropper. He has been a drawing account which has been startled to run around $300. per week. At the end of the year when Massa Mills' cotton has been laid by, Duke is told that he owes them hundreds of thousands of dollars . . . When they finish totaling, there aren't any profits . . .

Most of these conditions hold forth for the hide-ho master—Mr. Calloway occupying now

> That spring for me (and, I guess, all of us) was the end of the Harlem Renaissance. We were no longer in vogue, anyway, we Negroes. Sophisticated New Yorkers turned to Noel Coward. Colored actors began to go hungry, publishers politely rejected new manuscripts, and patrons found other uses for their money. The cycle that had charlestoned into being on the dancing heels of Shuffle Along now ended in Green Pastures with De Lawd.
>
> —Langston Hughes, The Big Sea

the highest spot on the Rialto, his men earning under $100 per week. Musical sharecroppers, that's all . . .

Now take Jimmie Lunceford and his men. They fell into Mills' snares in the early stages. They, too, were musical peons. Realising this they revolted. Mills had them bound by contract. They owed for their cabin, plot, mule and sorghum. But the boys pulled a fast one—they decided to buy their contracts . . .

Musical sharecropping doesn't just sing right to this grandpappy's son. The Negro has share-cropped too long . . . We don't want anymore paternalism on our job, we want a chance and a fair wage. And we'll take care of the rest.[4]

Unemployed men sitting on crates on the sidewalk, Harlem, 1939. (Museum of the City of New York)

While the working black musicians had their problems, the average Harlemites, the faceless numbers in Harlem's unemploy-ment statistics, were the ones who really felt trapped. They could not afford the prices in the white-owned Harlem stores; they could not even get jobs in them. They were hungry; they could not clothe their children; many could not even maintain a roof over their heads. Despair, anger, frus-tration and resentment boiled up inside them and on March 19, 1935, exploded.

Lino Rivera, a black Puerto Rican, went to a movie that afternoon. He did not have a job. After the movie, for want of anything else to do, he went to the Kress depart-ment store on 125th Street. There the six-teen-year-old spied a ten-cent knife, and having no money to buy it, slipped it into his pocket. He was immediately grabbed by a male employee of the store, and a scuffle ensued. A crowd of shoppers gath-ered, attracted by the noise. They were black and clearly on the side of the boy.

Yesterday
A night-gone thing
A sun-down name.

—Langston Hughes

When Rivera suddenly bit one of his captors on the thumb, the man shouted, "I'm going to take you down to the basement and beat hell out of you!"

It is hard to establish the exact chain of events that followed. Within moments, the rumor that a white man was beating a black boy to death spread through the streets of Harlem. And when the people heard an ambulance siren, there was no doubt in their minds that the rumor was true. While the ambulance had actually been summoned for the man with the bitten finger, the people of Harlem were sure that the boy had been brutally beaten. Someone threw a brick and then, like spontaneous combustion, Harlem exploded in a night of looting and burning such as had never been seen before.

The deepening resentment, born of the Depression, and the increased gang violence were casting a pall on the bright visage of Harlem. But there were other reasons for the tarnish on its image. It had been popular because it was new and different. Newness does not last; difference soon becomes commonplace. Black entertainers and musicians who had gained applause and acceptance elsewhere began to look upon Harlem not as "the top" but as the lowly beginning. White socialites were looking for new fads. Harlem was becoming a "has-been."

The Harlem Renaissance and the era of the New Negro ended as well. Some among the black intelligentsia had expected it. They had never believed the Harlem Renaissance represented a real and lasting gain in race relations anyway. Wallace Thurman was one. Over the years, his despair over the future of black Americans and his awareness that the Harlem Renaissance would indeed end had driven him to drink. He died in 1934. Rudolph Fisher was another. He died within a week of Thurman. Langston Hughes was still another. He greeted the end of the Harlem vogue with cynical acceptance. "The depression brought everybody down a peg or two," he wrote. "And the Negro had but few pegs to fall."[5]

The reasons for the demise of the Harlem Renaissance were as complex as the reasons for its inception, but the overwhelming factor here, too, was the Depression. It was the Depression that caused the increase in underworld violence and the smoldering anti-white resentment of many Harlemites. The shadow of the sordid world of the slum overcame the artificial light of the myth-Harlem. Though liquor was again legally available, the nation itself had sobered greatly; it no longer searched for dreamlands inhabited by people who sang and danced and laughed all day. The Negro passed from fashion.

The Cotton Club management hoped that it was Harlem itself, not the Negro per se, that had fallen from favor. The club had acquired a glamorous reptuation over the twelve years of its existence, and its owners were planning to transplant that glamour to a safer, more acceptable location.

The Harlem Cotton Club closed its doors for good on February 16, 1936. It was truly the end of an era.

Chapter 7

THE COTTON CLUB COMES TO BROADWAY

The site chosen for the downtown Cotton Club was ideal. It was a big room on the top floor of a building on Broadway and Forty-eighth Street, where Broadway and Seventh Avenue meet—an important midtown crossroads, and in the heart of the Great White Way, the Broadway theater district. Formerly occupied by the Palais Royal, the site had played host to the downtown Connie's Inn, renamed the Harlem Club, from 1933 to 1934. However, the Immerman brothers had changed more than the club's name. Feeling that the time was right, they opted for a club catering specifically to blacks. They were mistaken, and the club closed within a few months. It was replaced by the Ubangi Club, which offered a "pansy" show in which Gladys Bentley performed in a man's suit, with a top hat and cane. The Ubangi Club stayed open at that site for about a year, after which it moved farther down Broadway to the cellar that later became Birdland. The move opened

Opposite: Bill Robinson. (Culver Pictures)

the way for the Cotton Club to give the big room musical distinction once again.

The club's management went to considerable expense to redecorate their new home. Like the uptown club, it was heavily carpeted and terraced, and while a jungle décor similar to that of the uptown club was installed, the old cupid-strewn ceilings and "theater boxes" were retained. Some said the Cotton Club finally had the setting it should have enjoyed all along. After all, its revues had always been much closer to Broadway productions than to night-club shows.

While Herman Stark and the club's owners were quite certain the club would do well in its new location, they realized a lot depended on a smash-hit opening show, and they lined up the best talent they could find to ensure success. They could not have done better than with Bill "Bojangles" Robinson—and in his fiftieth year as a dancer at that.

Robinson is one of the most loved and respected performers in black entertainment history. Born in Richmond, Virginia, in May 1878, he began his dancing career at the age of eight, just at the time when

Bill Robinson playing Santa at the Cotton Club (with his wife, Elaine). (Museum of the City of New York)

blacks first started to appear in vaudeville. For years, Robinson did one-nighters and fill-in spots in small clubs and vaudeville theaters. In 1903, when he was twenty-five, he teamed up with a partner in the act Cooper and Robinson. When that partnership dissolved five years later, Robinson formed a new act with a man named Butler. After that, he decided to try again as a single performer, and with the help of the agent he chose at that time, Marty Forkins, he did. The two developed a deep friendship and loyalty for each other and continued their relationship until November 1949, when Robinson died.

Robinson got the idea for his stair dance in 1921. As an encore at the Palace, in New York, he danced up and down the stairs on the side of the stage that led down to the orchestra. Audience reaction was so great that he developed and refined the routine until it became his trademark. While not the originator of dancing on steps, his rendition was entirely original.

According to legend, Robinson received his nickname after an all-night poker game in Harlem. Robinson, a big winner in the game, got up and began a happy dance of victory. Des Williams, one of the losers, suddenly exclaimed, "Bojangles! That's what he is—he's Bojangles!" He was known by that name from then on.

Robinson rose to stardom on Broadway, in night clubs, and later in movies such as The Little Colonel, In Old Kentucky, The Littlest Rebel and Rebecca of Sunnybrook Farm. He staged the dances for the movie Dimples and taught Shirley Temple, among other great stars, dance routines. Meanwhile he achieved another kind of fame— as easily the most generous performer in the business. He played more benefits than any other entertainer. He rarely bothered to ask who or what a benefit was for; if it was a benefit, he figured it was doing

Bill Robinson and Cab Calloway entertaining at the Cotton Club. (Culver Pictures)

somebody some good. In Harlem during the Depression years a benefit performance without him was unheard of. He handed out thousands of Christmas baskets and grocery baskets, often for the Cotton Club. Once he sought to cheer up the poor by personally wrapping some of the packages and handing them out. But when people who received packages not wrapped by Robinson protested, the practice had to be discontinued. In a ceremony complete with speeches by prominent Harlemites, Robinson was named to the honorary office of "Mayor of Harlem."

Cab Calloway received equal billing for the first downtown Cotton Club show. By 1936 he had become a superstar in his own right. To ensure a crowd-drawing show, it had been arranged that Calloway would revive his "Minnie the Moocher," and he presented the number every night for the duration of the show.

Top stars were only part of the show's success. The behind-the-scenes talent was equally important, and Stark and Healy had seen to that as well. Benny Davis and J. Fred Coots wrote the songs. While not an Arlen and Koehler, or a McHugh and Fields, this team was talented and highly successful. Clarence Robinson choreographed the dances, Julian Harrison designed the sets, Billy Weaver and Veronica designed and executed the costumes. Easily the most important acquisition to the staff was Will Vodery for orchestration. Vodery, a quiet, dignified man, had been Florenz Ziegfeld's arranger from 1911 to 1932. After Ziegfeld's death in 1932 he had worked for Rudolf Friml, Jerome Kern and Fox Films. He added subtle and imaginative dimensions to the Cotton Club music, and he stayed with the club for a number of years.

The most lavish revue in the Cotton Club's thirteen-year history opened on Broadway on September 24, 1936. Robinson and Calloway headed a roster of some 130 other performers, among them Avis Andrews, the Berry Brothers, Katherine Perry, Whyte's Maniacs, the Tramp Band, Anne Lewis, Dynamite Hooker, Wen Talbert's Choir, the Bahama Dancers, Broadway

Jones and the exotic dancer Kaloah. "Black Magic," "Copper Colored Gal," "I'm at the Mercy of Love" and "Hi-de-Ho Miracle Man" were among the numbers that were featured.

The Cotton Club Boys had temporarily broken up after the club closed in Harlem. Six of them had continued the act and were booked into New York, Washington, Baltimore and Philadelphia theaters doing their old routines. Like other performers before them, they found that the Cotton Club name opened many doors. When the fall 1936 show premiered at the downtown Cotton Club, however, the Cotton Club Boys were back, and with the Cotton Club Girls they introduced the Susie-Q, which quickly became the latest dance craze.

A bit rough and not quite as fast as it should have been on opening night, the show, like most shows, was refined on succeeding nights, the rough spots smoothed out, the pace quickened. It was, as Variety would have put it, a socko show.

Lured by the show and by the new, more easily accessible location, the crowds flocked to the Cotton Club, which did a turnaway business for the dinner and supper shows. In the third week alone, the club grossed more than $45,000, and in the first sixteen weeks the average weekly gross receipts topped $30,000.

Prices were a little higher at the Cotton Club now than they had been in the early thirties, but then, prices were higher everywhere. The Steak Sandwich, $1.25 before, was now $2.25; Scrambled Eggs, Deerfoot Sausage had risen only a quarter, to $1.50; earlier, lobster and crabmeat cocktails were $1.00 each, now they were $1.50 and $1.25, respectively. Olives, on the other hand, had gone down; a side order, which had once cost 50 cents, now could be had

for 40 cents. The most expensive dish on the Chinese portion of the menu, Moo Goo Guy Pan, was still $2.25. Other 1936 prices: Baked Oyster Cotton Club—$1.75; Broiled Filet Mignon, French Fried Potatoes—$3; Broiled Live Lobster—$2.50 and up; Egg Foo Young—$1.50. One notable price reduction was the club's cover charge. Anywhere from $2.50 to $3 in the Harlem days, on Broadway it was $1.50 to $2 table d'hote dinner policy, and no cover charge thereafter. Logically, now that the club had moved away from a neighborhood inhabited by Negro undesirables, it was no longer necessary to maintain a high cover charge to keep them out. Relatively few blacks crossed the "Mason-Dixon Line" of 110th Street.

All in all, the Broadway Cotton Club was a highly successful blend of old and new. Having learned from the failure of the downtown Connie's Inn, the Cotton Club people made few changes in their successful uptown formula. The site may have been new, the décor may have been slightly different, but once a patron entered and was comfortably seated, he knew he was in a familiar place. If the former titillating hint of danger associated with the Harlem location was no more, the sense of "rubbing elbows with the mob" was still there. Herman Stark was always

Possibly interior of Connie's Inn. (Schomburg Collection, NYPL)

The Cotton Club

around, chomping on a cigar and surveying his domain, and Frenchy DeMange could generally be found at his favorite table receiving visitors or playing cards.

"I used to drop into the Cotton Club after it had shifted activities to West Forty-eighth Street from its former Harlem site," columnist Louis Sobol later recalled, "and engage in pinochle duels with Big Frenchy DeMange, one of the formidable chieftains of gangdom. They were serious battles, and Frenchy would get apoplectic when he lost, though the stakes were minimal. But once the session was over, he became a good-natured host, and it was difficult to conceive that this big burly man had been on the Public Enemy roster."[1]

Another major attraction at the Cotton Club that season was the celebration of Bill Robinson's fiftieth year in show business at midnight, December 12, 1936. Herman Stark had arranged a star-studded and highly sentimental tribute to Robinson, a rather unique one at which, as Ed Sullivan commented in his column the following week, "Broadway laid aside all its cheapness and meanness, and let its hair down to join in . . . ."

Dan Healy and Cab Calloway co-hosted the event. Ethel Merman sang, as did Aunt Jemima. Jim Barton, Block and Sully, and Ted Husing made appearances. Johnson and Dean, famous for originating the cakewalk, danced it again before ringside tables filled with famous faces. Darryl Zanuck had sent a wire from Hollywood, and Shirley Temple an affectionate telegram. Alfred Lunt, Noel Coward, Mayor Fiorello LaGuardia, Fred Astaire, Ray Bolger, Max Schmeling and others made speeches. Through all of it, Robinson beamed with pleasure.

Then Dan Healy began to present the gifts that the Cotton Club kids—members of the chorus, Cotton Club Girls and Boys—had bought for Robinson and his wife. The

gift presentation over, he was called to the microphone at 3:45 A.M. Bojangles' smile faded. As he started to speak, the tears streamed down his cheeks, and he walked off the floor with a handkerchief to his eyes. It was a more eloquent gesture than any speech he could have made.

Despite their careful planning, Stark and the Cotton Club owners were surprised at the great success of their first revue on Broadway. They were just as careful to plan for the spring 1937 show, and it proved to be an even greater triumph. What made its success particularly gratifying for blacks in show business was that it was the first show for which all the major numbers were written by blacks—Ellington, Andy Razaf, John Redmond and Reginald Forsythe.

For Ellington it was a triumphal return. In the ten years since the band had first opened at the Cotton Club uptown it had achieved international acclaim, and had just returned from some film assignments in Hollywood. Ivy Anderson had more than a little to do with the band's success. She was one of the most exciting female band singers around. She had appeared in Shuffle Along, and in 1931 had been working as the featured singer at the Grand Café in Chicago when she was asked to work with Duke at the Oriental Theatre in that city. She remained with the Ellington band for some ten years. She had accompanied the band to England in 1933, along with dancer Bessie Dudley, and had achieved considerable acclaim abroad.

The first record Ivy Anderson made with Ellington was "It Don't Mean a Thing If It Ain't Got That Swing," an Ellington composition. It was the first song to use the term swing for jazz. Swing, in jazz lingo, is a way of playing; there is a lift and a propelling beat that is highly distinguishable to the

Opposite: Ivy Anderson. (Collection of Duncan Schiedt)

jazz-familiar ear. The song was an instant hit, and it "made" Ivy Anderson. After that, Ellington and his band continued to rise in fame, but without Ivy Anderson there would definitely have been something missing.

Stark did not rely on the Ellington band alone to draw crowds. He lined up a talent-packed cast of performers to share top billing. In fact, the show was the first, at the Cotton Club or anywhere else, to star so many top black performers in one production. Ethel Waters was back, having just completed a tour of West Coast night clubs. Back, too, was George Dewey Washington. And the popular young dance team the Nicholas Brothers were making their first appearance at the Cotton Club.

Fayard and Harold Nicholas grew up in the business. Their parents had been the leaders of an orchestra, a forerunner of the name bands that became popular in the late twenties and early thirties. The brothers began their dancing career in 1928, when they were ten and seven, respectively, appearing as an added attraction to a popular vaudeville bill on the stage of the Strand Theatre in Philadelphia, where their parents were playing. By 1937, when they arrived at the Cotton Club, they were already quite successful. In fact, they traveled to New York aboard the Queen Mary after a triumphant engagement in London. But their appearance at the downtown Cotton Club was, as Harold later recalled, "our first real break." They remained with the club for five years.

The revue's official title was the Cotton Club Express, and it was the fastest show the club had ever presented. The opening set featured the rear observation platform of a train, and baritone George Dewey Washington, garbed as a train announcer, promised a show that "would corner," as

Ed Sullivan wrote the following day, "the hi-de-ho and ho-de-ho market."

Harold Nicholas of the Nicholas Brothers did some fast-paced hoofing to "Tap Is Tops," which gave way to Kaloah's wriggling to Ellington's "Black and Tan Fantasy." Anise and Aland executed a graceful waltz number, followed by a

Ivy and Duke. (Collection of Duncan Schiedt)

Bill Robinson at the Orpheum. (Culver Pictures)

dance specialty by a new group, the Three Giants of Rhythm. Then Ethel Waters, supported by a background of beautifully gowned chorus girls, sang what was planned as the major song of the show, "Where Is the Sun?" written by John Redmond and Lee David.

The revue was packed with dance numbers. The Nicholas Brothers did a specialty number, followed by the Cotton Club's bow to the growing South American influence in U.S. dancing. It was an ambitious production number called "Chile," sung by Ivy Anderson, and danced not only by Anise and Aland but also by Renee and Estela, a rhumba team whom Stark had gotten from the Club Yumuri especially for the number. Bessie Dudley shook her hips to Ellington's "Rockin' in Rhythm," and Bill Bailey tapped out "Tap Mathemetician."

Then the tempo shifted. Ethel Waters came onstage to do some of the songs that she had made, and that had made her, famous—"Stormy Weather," "Happiness Is Just a Thing Called Joe." It was in this performance, less formal than the lavish "Where Is the Sun?" production, that she was at her best. As one columnist put it: " . . . when you encounter her striking interpretations of some songs ranging from her classic 'Stormy Weather' to Cole Porter's sardonic 'Miss Otis Regrets,' you will see that she is, among other things, a truly creative player. She dominates the performance, dominates it with her unflagging spirit, her casual splendor and her instinctive theatrical wisdom, and I suspect that, even without the other virtues of the evening, she, splendidly accompanied by her brother on the piano and her husband on a muted cornet, would revive for you all the glories of a fine tradition."[2] (The columnist was either misinformed or just being

polite in calling the trumpet player, Eddie Mallory, Ethel's husband. Her half-brother, Johnny, played piano with Mallory's band for a while.)

As a finale Mae Diggs, the Nicholas Brothers and the chorus, dressed in chicken costumes, introduced "peckin'," billed as the new dance craze to succeed the Susie-Q. At first the tune, "Peckin'," was properly credited to Ellington, for it came straight out of Cootie Williams' solo in "Rockin' in Rhythm."

The show was a smash—lively, fast-paced and, to quote Ed Sullivan once again, "easily the most elegant colored show Broadway has ever applauded."

Eddie Mallory. (Collection of Duncan Schiedt)

Among the first-night customers were Sylvia Sidney, Lou Holtz, and physician Dr. Leo Michel, known among theatrical people as Dr. Broadway, and they were among the lucky. From the very first night the club was turning away crowds, and by the fourth week the show had played to over 50,000 persons, breaking all previous club records. Anticipating receipts that would come close to the million-dollar mark, Herman Stark quickly moved to extend the show's run and to make sure its stars would remain with it until it closed. In mid-April the happy announcement came—both Ellington and Ethel Waters had agreed to postpone previous commitments to assure continuance of the lavish revue until June 15.

One night Leopold Stokowski came in and sat, alone, in one of the boxes. Ellington noticed the white-haired conductor and walked over and introduced himself.

Stokowski rose to meet him. "I have always wanted to meet you and hear you conduct your compositions," he said.

"This is one of the proudest moments of my life. I've always had the greatest admiration for you," Ellington said.

"Tell me," Stokowski continued, "what are you striving for in your music?"

"I am endeavoring to establish unadulterated Negro melody portraying the American Negro," Duke explained. And then he proceeded to illustrate, leading the band through a medley of his concertos.

Stokowski applauded loudly. "Mr. Ellington," he said, "now I truly understand the Negro soul."[3]

The conductor then invited Ellington to his concert at Carnegie Hall the following evening, and Duke had the honor of sitting alone in a box at Carnegie, while, as columnist Louis Sobol put it, "the Caucasian conductor led his vast orchestra [the Philadelphia] in an interpretation of the vague white-folks' soul."

Ethel Waters and Tom Dorsey of the Dorsey brothers' orchestra. (Culver Pictures)

Sobol's comment indicates that for some, at least, the idea that the Negro soul was somehow purer and truer than the white persisted. But these some were now fast approaching a minority. So, too, were those whites who opted for the complex rhythms of Negro jazz as opposed to the sounds of swing. In 1936 the ''swing era'' had begun in America, with large white bands like that of Benny Goodman bringing jazz to a much wider public. The same columnist quoted earlier who praised Ethel Waters in the show also praised Ellington, but appended the following: ''I trust that you approve of him [Ellington] and his orchestra—just as I trust, incidentally, that you are an enthusiast for Benny Goodman and his associates.'' It was a movement that Ellington, for one, cared little for. He took to making a strong distinction between his work and that of the so-called swing bands.

Chapter 8

Herman Stark signed Bill Robinson and Cab Calloway to costar in the fall 1937 show, the third to be presented at the club in its Broadway location. In order to get Robinson, Stark had to make special arrangements with Darryl F. Zanuck and Twentieth Century-Fox, with whom Robinson was under contract and for whom he had done <u>The Littlest Rebel</u> with Shirley Temple in 1936. Stark also agreed to pay Robinson $3,500 a week, the highest salary ever paid a black entertainer in a Broadway production, and more money than had ever been received by <u>any</u> individual for a night-club appearance.

One week before the opening, however, Zanuck called Robinson to Hollywood to do <u>Rebecca of Sunnybrook Farm</u> with Shirley Temple, which caused a bit of consternation at the Cotton Club. Because much of the show had been built around Robinson, the decision was made to delay the opening of the show for a

Opposite: Ann Pennington. (Museum of the City of New York)

couple of weeks, during which time the Nicholas Brothers could rehearse to replace Robinson.

The show that finally opened suffered very little from Robinson's absence. Large, lavish and fast-paced, it featured (in addition to Calloway and the Nicholas Brothers) Avis Andrews, Mae Johnson, Dynamite Hooker, the Three Choclateers, the Tramp Band, Will Vodery's Jubileers, James Skelton, Freddy James, fifty showgirls and six Cotton Club Boys. Benny Davis and J. Fred Coots wrote the score of twelve songs, among them "Tall, Tan and Terrific," "Nightfall in Louisiana" and "I'm in the Mood for You." Perhaps the best parts of the show were those that featured sixteen-year-old Harold Nicholas, who mastered in five days the routines abandoned by Robinson and received tumultuous applause on opening night and every succeeding night.

The traditional jungle effects were provided by Tip, Tap & Toe dancing on top of a large wooden drum, and by the sensuous dancing of Tondelayo, Princess Orelia and Engagi.

Mae Johnson did a hilariously funny take-off on Mae West in the song "I'm a Lady," and Cab Calloway, as usual, was energetic enough to carry the entire show. In his funniest number, "Hi-De-Ho Romeo," Calloway, dressed in doublets, played Romeo to Mae Johnson's Juliet in swing-time. The entire cast danced to a catchy and memorable number, "Harlem Bolero."

Once again Stark had employed his winning formula, and as one columnist put it, the resulting revue proved that it was "greater than any individual star." Indeed, concerned that the loss of Robinson would result in a rather small attendance, Stark had at first presented only the after-dinner

Cotton Club beauties, including Lena Horne. (Collection of Duncan Schiedt)

and after-theater shows. But with a hit show on his hands, after all, and throngs of crowds coming to the club, Stark announced that an extra revue would be offered every night at 2:30 A.M., featuring the entire cast.

Of all people, the master of ceremonies for the fall show of 1937, along with host Dan Healy, was Connie Immerman. Whatever else might have been said about the Cotton Club management, they never failed to help out "one of their own."

When Bill Robinson returned to the Cotton Club, the Nicholas Brothers went back on the road, and the club closed for a few days in order to rehearse some new specialty acts and to re-center the show around Robinson. This meant lost revenues, of course, and Stark was privately unhappy with the changes the club and cast had been forced to go through as a result of Robinson's sudden departure and subsequent return, the special agreement with Twentieth Century-Fox notwithstanding. Also, there was the matter of Robinson's extraordinary salary.

Robinson, however, was prepared to make a gesture in return, for the new version of the show would feature a new dance, the Bill Robinson Walk. It was the first dance he had created in over fifty years in show business that he considered expressive enough to carry his name. Needless to say, the Bill Robinson Walk was eagerly awaited.

The Cotton Club management, costumers and choreographers outdid themselves on the number. Fifty chorus girls appeared with Robinson in rubber Bojangles masks, and their movements echoed and counterpointed his own in a performance that brought many in the audience to their feet.

Thus, despite its late start and its midseason changes, the latest Cotton Club Parade was highly successful among both

columnists and audiences. Here and there, however, columnists expressed weariness with Stark's winning formula. As one by-lineless column said about the show:

. . . That it's overboard on hoofing is a common failing of Negro floor shows, and is explained away by the obvious fact that any "serious" singing doesn't seem to be accepted by the ofay trade; also a fast dancing pace is most consistently successful formula.

As a sidelight on this, one wonders what would be the result if they ever got away from the same routine of torrid terping; a coocher (usually backgrounded by a Congo motif); double-entendre lyrics (Ethel Waters started that vogue, and that takes in all the sundry switches on the "Pool Table Papa" school of lyricizing); a "new" dance (Suzi-Q, truckin', peckin', etc.); and the cavalcade of standard Negro fol-de-rol. But Herman Stark, impresario of the Cotton Club, both uptown and in midtown, has found from many years of experience just what pays, so what price glory?[1]

Duke Ellington and his orchestra returned to the Cotton Club to rehearse for the spring 1938 show. He had been named by Life magazine one of the "Twenty Most Prominent Negroes in the United States." Soon (in late February) he was to be part of a "High-Low" concert at the Viennese Roof on the posh St. Regis, where he was the hit of the evening. By now he was what might be called a "polite success" in polite society, but he was a sensation among the Broadway crowd.

Ellington was looking forward to the new Cotton Club show, which would have even more supporting acts than the previous Broadway site shows and would be a full two hours in length. For the first time he would be writing the entire score, with the collaboration of fine lyricists, foremost among whom was Henry Nemo, one of the true characters of the New York entertainment world. At 250 pounds, he was literally

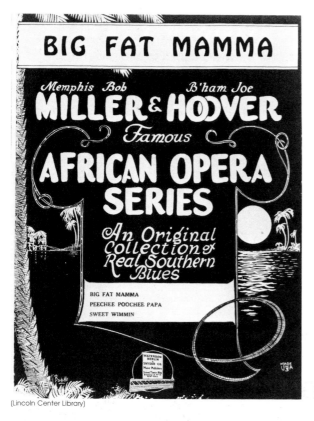

BIG FAT MAMMA

Memphis Bob   B'ham Joe
MILLER & HOOVER
Famous
AFRICAN OPERA
SERIES
An Original
Collection of
Real Southern
Blues

BIG FAT MAMMA
PEECHEE POOCHEE PAPA
SWEET WIMMIN

(Lincoln Center Library)

a barrel of laughs. Singer, dancer, comedian, songwriter, he would entertain anywhere, anytime. Also, he was one of the few personalities who actually spoke the way the Broadway columnists wrote—that particular brand of fast-talk that incorporated such words as "socko," "hoi polloi" and many more up-tempo words and phrases. His favorite self-description: "The Neem is on the Beam."

Yet beneath the clown exterior beat a keenly sensitive heart—Nemo was capable of writing the most softly romantic lyrics. " 'Tis Autumn" and "Don't Take Your Love from Me" are Nemo songs. Ellington, who was trying his hand at love ballads for the first time, and Nemo together produced two memorable torch songs, "If You Were in My Place" and "I Let a Song Go Out of My Heart," which proved to be among the three masterpieces of the show.

The latter number almost did not get written. Working with Nemo and other lyricists, first on one tune, then on another, back and forth, seeing song after song materialize, Ellington was almost taken by surprise when he realized that twelve tunes had been completed. The others were satisfied with the output, but Ellington was not. Extremely superstitious, he decided that a show with twelve numbers was unlucky. Enlisting Nemo's help, he composed the thirteenth, "I Let a Song Go Out of My Heart."

Rehearsals for the show gave Ellington the opportunity to renew his acquaintance with Will Vodery, with whom he had worked in Florenz Ziegfeld's Show Girl after leaving the Cotton Club in 1930. George Gershwin had written the score for Show Girl, and while the show did not give Ellington any opportunities to exhibit his own composing talents, it had given both him and his orchestra much-needed experience. Ellington learned much from Vodery, who was then Ziegfeld's arranger. Ellington had been exposed to little traditional music. Vodery had. Vodery had assimilated the classical experience and translated it into a successful comedy, pit-band style. It was much easier for Ellington to understand the harmonies and colorations of classical music in this translated form, and Ellington often credited Vodery with teaching him orchestration. During the late winter and early spring of 1938, while rehearsing for the new Cotton Club show, Ellington and Vodery reminisced a lot about Show Girl and the Ziegfeld days.

The show opened at midnight on Thursday, March 9, 1938, and it was yet another hit for Herman Stark. In addition to the two popular songs written with Nemo, Ellington's "Braggin' in Brass" brought the audience to its feet, and "A Lesson in C" satisfied the patrons' desire for a bit of symphonic jazz. The "swingtime Romeo and

Juliet'' act of the previous show had been such a success that Mae Johnson continued it without Cab Calloway. Her hilarious Mae West impersonation in the act occasioned the first night club appearance since achieving movie stardom of the real Mae West, who was guest of honor at one of the club's Sunday ''celebrity nights.'' Anise and Aland, Aida Ward, the Four Step Brothers and the Three Choclateers did their specialties. The Peters Sisters, who had appeared in numerous motion pictures, made their New York night-club debut in the show. Weighing 300 pounds each, they commandeered the stage with their singing and dancing in ''Swingtime in Honolulu'' and ''Posin'.'' Another two-man dancing team was introduced—Rufus, seven, and Richard, five.

Among the most popular ''specialty act'' performers was Peg-Leg Bates, who was a star before he arrived at the Cotton Club, although his stint there certainly did not hurt his career. Peg-Leg, whose real name is Clayton, got his name because he actually has a wooden leg. In 1918, at the age of ten, he was working in a cotton mill in Greenville, South Carolina. One night the little boy slid into the auger of a cotton-seed mill and lost his left leg. While most people would have considered such an accident tragic, Bates recalls that night as the luckiest of his life. ''Hadn't been for that,'' he says, ''I'd be on a cotton farm this minute, plowing my crop.''[2]

A small boy with only one leg is open to much sympathy and a great deal of ridicule, neither of which set very well with

> play my people
> all my people who breathe
> the breath of the earth
> all my people who are keys
>   and chords
>
> make chords that speak
> play long play soft
>
> —Henry Dumas

Clayton Bates. He got his uncle to make him a peg leg and he practiced on it, in the woods by himself, until he could walk and run five miles at a stretch.

"Then one night," Bates recalls, "my uncle was in the kitchen at home. He had just come back from the war, and he was in good spirits. He began to dance on the kitchen floor. I got up and imitated him. I found I could make a beat and match it with my peg. I got ambitious."[3]

Soon he was dancing in the amateur shows at the Liberty, a black theater in Greenville, where he won prize after prize. When a stock show came through town, he ran away with it. He played across the South, with one company after another, sometimes as an individual act and sometimes as part of a team. He arrived in New York in 1928 to play a week at the Lafayette Theatre in Harlem, and he attracted such attention that Lew Leslie signed him for Blackbirds of 1928. After accompanying the show to Paris, he returned to New York to play at the Paradise (downtown) and Connie's Inn. Two trips

to London and he was back in New York, stomping out on the Cotton Club stage and singing, "I'm Peg-Leg Bates, that one-legged dancing fool." He now owned "thirteen peg-legs, one to fit every suit, all colors . . ."

In the spring of 1938 Cotton Club show he danced to "Slappin' Seventh Avenue with the Sole of My Shoe," and audience applause brought him back on the stage more than any other performer.

After Bates's number, the chorus danced to "Carnival in Caroline," and in the grand finale the company introduced yet another new dance, the skrontch, which, it was said, had been done a century earlier in Kentucky. While it was not as exciting as earlier dances introduced at the club, its "catchy" name would ensure it long life. Later, in recording, the name would be made a little less catchy, changed to " the scrounch," for obvious reasons.

The names of Ellington's tunes were quite frequently questioned, or changed for mass consumption, although sometimes those that were questioned need not have

> The Cotton Club was an exotic, jungle-like café. The shows had a primitive naked quality that was supposed to make a cilivized audience lose its inhibitions.
>
> —Lena Horne

been and those that were not questioned should have been. April 29, 1938, marked Ellington's thirty-ninth birthday and approximately his tenth year in the music business, and the Cotton Club celebrated with a matinee party and a special broadcast to England through the BBC. As was the usual procedure, the numbers for the broadcast were submitted to the censor board for clearance and were passed. But just before the scheduled broadcast, a worried assistant called from the station to question the titles of two numbers, "Hip Chick" and "Dinah's in a Jam." Did the former have anything to do with hips? And it was hoped that the latter title did not refer to pregnancy. Ned E. Williams, publicity man for Ellington's agent Irving Mills, assured both the assistant and the now-worried censor board that they had nothing to worry about, but he could not allay their fears. As both numbers were instrumentals, it was decided to give them tamer titles for the broadcast. Interestingly enough, the radio censors never questioned the meanings of such titles as "T. T. on Toast," "Warm Valley," and others.

Before the opening of the fall 1938 show, the Cotton Club was redecorated. Julian Harrison, former scenic designer for Cecil B. DeMille and who had been associated with the club for some years, supervised the decorations, which included the redesigning of the bar and entrance lounge and the installation of murals depicting the evolution of swing.

By this time, swing had completely captured the public taste, and the major white swing bands overshadowed all but the most successful black bands such as Ellington's and Calloway's. Aware of the popularity of swing and always quick to capitalize on a trend, the club's manage-

Duke Ellington and Ethel Waters. (Museum of the City of New York)

ment commissioned the murals. Among the bandleaders who appeared there were Benny Goodman, Tommy Dorsey, Gene Krupa and Larry Clinton, but in the Cotton Club murals their likenesses were given what surely would have been called, in those days, a "sepian twist." They were all depicted in blackface.

The club also elaborated its service by installing for the first time a maître d' in the person of one Robert Collins.

Cab Calloway was brought back for the show; this alternation of Ellington's and Calloway's bands was becoming something of a tradition. Calloway shared top billing with the Nicholas Brothers, and together they presided over the usually talent-packed roster of performers including the Berry Brothers, Mae Johnson, Whyte's Lindy Hoppers, the Cotton Club Boys, and June Richmond. W. C. Handy, famous for "St. Louis Blues," would appear from time to time to play trumpet or cornet in the finale, but he did not play every show. While still active and energetic, he was getting on in years. On November 20 the club held a gala celebration to mark his sixty-fifth birthday.

The show opened on September 28, the curtain lifting to reveal a plantation setting—"Col. Cosgrove's Plantation" said the identifying sign—with a decidedly thirties

Benny Davis. (Lincoln Center Library)

air. Other signs prominently displayed on either side of the stage read: MY BOSS STILL HAS THE FIRST DAME HE EVER MADE! and SILK UNDERWEAR DON'T MAKE A LADY. However, there was neither a plantation nor any other unifying theme for the show, which was a potpourri of fast-paced entertainment, heavy on dancing and light on comedy.

Benny Davis and J. Fred Coots had written the score, which included such songs as "I've Got a Heart Full of Rhythm" and "Scarlet O'Hara from Seventh Avenue." The latter, sung by Mae Johnson, poked fun at David O. Selznick and Clark Gable in its ribald lyrics, and was one of the big hits of the show.

Jigsaw Jackson did an acrobatic-contortionistic dance, Estralita shimmied

while Mae Johnson sang "Congo Conga," and Cab Calloway led the number "A Lesson in Jive." A new dance, the boogie-woogie, was introduced, and because Cuban dancing was all the rage, the club featured, in addition to the "Congo Conga" number, a new dance band, Toc-cares' Orchestra, billed as from Cuba.

Two "new acts" were presented in the show. Of the two, the more successful was Sister Rosetta Tharpe, who presented the first Holy Roller-gospel numbers ever featured at the club. Already fairly well established as a folk celebrity, Sister Tharpe had risen to prominence on the crest of the popular gospel-music wave. Long considered particular, and peculiar, to Southern churches, gospel had been introduced to Northern blacks by Mahalia Jackson and others in the twenties. Northern black ministers and other bourgeois blacks considered gospel a dirty word, but despite their objections the style had flourished. It had not taken long for clever entrepreneurs to see the commercial possibilities in gospel, and a split occurred among gospel singers. On one side were those like Mahalia Jackson, who believed that gospel was God's music and that to turn it into a show for night club drinkers was to mock God's work. On the other side were those like Clara Ward who believed there was a place for "pop gospel"; good sentiments were the same whether expressed in church or cabaret, and if people were willing to pay to hear them, so much the better. Rosetta Tharpe was of the latter opinion, although she was a good friend of Mahalia Jackson's. At the Cotton Club, Sister Tharpe gave lively interpretations of "Hallelujah Brown," "Rock Me" and "The Preacher," and her guitar playing alone

The Dandridge Sisters. (Earl Mills)

made a trip to the club to see the show well worth it.

The other "new act," the Dandridge Sisters, had arrived in New York after playing bit parts in several Hollywood movies—Going Places, Snow Gets in Your Eyes and It Can't Last Forever. Dorothy and Vivian Dandridge and the non-sister, Etta, were very young; Dorothy was only fourteen. In their style and in the type of songs they sang they were much like the Andrews Sisters. They were also quite naïve, having been brought up in the West and having a very protective agent, Joe Glaser. Dorothy Dandridge recalled when they sang their first number at a Cotton Club rehearsal:

The entire Cotton Club company was at hand during the rehearsal as Vivian, Etta, and I whipped through a number we believed was appropriate. It was all about,

"The midnight train came whoosin through,
The merrymakers were in full swing,
And everybody started to sing,
Da-da-de-um-dum-do."

The whole company broke into a fit of laughter that embarrassed us and cut us short. We figured we were finished.[4]

They were wrong, of course. They hadn't been brought all the way from the West Coast merely to audition. Their youth and their light-skinned good looks were what Stark was after. In the show they sang "A-Tisket A-Tasket" and "Swing Low, Sweet Chariot" and were featured with Calloway and June Richmond in "Madly in Love." Columnists called their style "refreshingly unique," and, one writer remarked, "with the middle femme especially strong vocally."

The "middle femme," Dorothy, was two years younger than Lena Horne had been

Dorothy Dandridge and Harold Nicholas. (Collection of Earl Mills)

when she joined the Cotton Club, and she was equally in awe of the older chorus girls, intrigued by their lives. She recalled:

They shelled out money on the perfume man and the lingerie man and the other special salesmen who came backstage. How could they afford all this? I wasn't that young; I suspected that not all of their purchases were made on a chorus girl's income. Between shows their boy friends came around. Limousines rolled up in back of the Club as if it was a bus terminal.[5]

Soon Dorothy was to have a boyfriend of her own—Harold Nicholas. "I saw Harold on the day I arrived at the Club," she later recalled. "We were backstage, making ready to put on our singing act for Cab Calloway and his men. Harold was on stage with his brother, Fayard, and they were doing a dance turn. As Harold tapped he was eyeing me. I had heard of him, had seen photos of him, and I knew that he and his brother were already famous and money-making entertainers . . . I learned that they had a big car and a chauffeur, and that their mother, who traveled with them, had a mink coat. All of which was impressive to a fourteen-year-old suddenly in the company of big-timers."[6]

Equally impressive was the seventeen-year-old Harold's talent. In the fall 1938 Cotton Club show he was revealed as a particularly creative performer, reminiscent in many ways of a young Bill Robinson. Columnists singled him out, something they

The Cotton Club

had not done before; and when he, in turn, singled out Dorothy, she was excited and flattered.

It did not take long for word of the romance to get around behind the scenes at the Cotton Club, and Dorothy noticed that the chorus girls gave her more than the usual number of worried looks. They were quite protective of her in general, ceasing their talk about men, for example, when she walked by. After she and Harold began seeing each other, she suspected they were talking about her, and she knew it when they hushed each other as she passed. Finally, one day, Mae Johnson exclaimed to the others, "Oh, don't be silly. Dotty's got to grow up. She might as well know."[7]

Dorothy Dandridge wanted to know. "They said that one girl who had been going with Harold had been so badly upset by a breakoff between them that she had had a nervous breakdown. I heard that Harold had been out with many of the girls in the company."[8]

Harold, Dorothy learned, had "been down the line," as the other girls put it. While only three years older than she, he was a decade beyond her in worldliness. She was warned to stay away from him, that he would get her into trouble. But Dorothy loved Harold, and Harold presented to her a very different side than he had shown to the other girls at the club whom he had dated. "It was a puritanical, idyllic relationship," Dorothy later recalled, "a four-year romance replete with talk-talk, hot dogs, movies, chitlins, boxes of candy, long walks, hand-holding, flowers. It was corny as the stalks in Iowa; and our sex was limited to kissing and getting hot, but for me it was fun."

A few years later Harold Nicholas became Dorothy Dandridge's first husband, but the marriage, like many in show business, was a brief and unhappy one.

Chapter 9

In 1939 the World's Fair came to New York for the first time since the Exhibition of the Industry of All Nations in the Crystal Palace in 1853–1854. Since then there had been world's fairs in other cities, like Chicago and Philadelphia, but New York had viewed the entire world's-fair concept with serene indifference. The city had neither the time nor the space for such gaudy nonsense. What happened to change the city's attitude is hard to determine. Perhaps the Depression had something to do with it, or perhaps it was the success of Chicago's Century of Progress in 1934 that jostled New York out of its lofty complacency. Whatever the reason, the city threw itself into preparations for the biggest world's fair ever. Its theme: Building the World of Tomorrow. Eighteen nations were represented when the fair opened on April 30, 1939.

The fair became the focal point of slick advertising campaigns, the gimmick for new products and for old products looking for a

Opposite: Jimmie Lunceford and orchestra members. (Culver Pictures)

new image. There was still the sense of wonder that a "world's fair" was feasible, that modern technological advances and modern travel could make possible a cooperative exposition among a group of countries separated by thousands of miles. For New Yorkers, in addition, it was a chance to celebrate their city. For other Americans, it was a reason to travel to the Big Apple, to see the things they had always heard about. Throughout the country, the World's Fair engendered considerably more excitement than any subsequent exposition.

Naturally, the show that opened at the Cotton Club at midnight on Friday, March 24, 1939, was billed as the World's Fair Edition of the Cotton Club Parade, although there was nothing in the show that was particularly related to the events out in Flushing Meadows, Queens. The club had been spruced up for the World's Fair season. The stage had been enlarged, and the orchestra area had been lowered from the dance-floor level, giving both stage and floor a more theatrical setting. The show was as talent-packed as Herman Stark could manage.

Duke Ellington's orchestra would have been a natural for the Cotton Club's World's Fair Edition. After all, Ellington had contributed to the club's international renown, and vice versa. But Ellington was unavailable, having been booked into a tour abroad to begin in March. Even if he had been available, Ellington would probably not have cared to book into the Cotton Club. Such a stint demanded a bit more dazzle than Ellington could likely have mustered at the time. He was going through some serious changes that spring, both in his professional and in his personal life.

Professionally, he had taken the great step of leaving Irving Mills. For years, outsiders had criticized Mills's relationship with his clients, charging, as Adam Clayton Powell had put it, that he made his clients "musical sharecroppers." Ellington had always brushed these criticisms aside, explaining that he was grateful to Mills for early financial support and wise business counsel. By late 1938–early 1939, however, Ellington

Sunday night at the Cotton Club was the night. All the big New York stars in town, no matter where they were playing, showed up at the Cotton Club to take bows.

—Duke Ellington, Music Is My Mistress

had begun to feel that he wasn't getting the attention he deserved from Mills, who managed Calloway as well as close to a dozen other groups, large and small. Ellington was disgruntled, but he might not have broken with Mills if he had not decided one afternoon to go to Mills's office to look at his books. Biographer Barry Ulanov reported:

Duke sat down at the table and looked through all the books of Duke Ellington, Incorporated, the record of his business association with Irving Mills. He looked at almost every page, at some with greater interest than others, at the reports on his best-selling records and those which hadn't sold so well, at the results of this theater booking and that location stand, the Cotton Clubs, East and West, Europe and short stands from coast to American coast.

"Thank you very much," Duke said to the secretary, after better than an hour's poring over the books of Duke Ellington Inc. He got up slowly, adjusted his jacket and tie, put on his hat and overcoat and walked out of the office. He never returned. In the spring of 1939, Duke signed a contract with William Morris, the oldest and greatest of the vaudeville and radio booking agencies, at that time making a belated entrance into the band business.[1]

A break in Ellington's personal life also occurred in 1939. For the past couple of years there had been many strains on Duke, and he and Mildred were not talking things over as they once had. While they still loved each other, they had lost something they could not regain, or that Duke, at least, did not want to make the effort to regain. During one of his earlier bookings at the Cotton Club, Duke had met chorus girl Bea Ellis, who made no attempt to hide the fact that she was crazy about him. Initially Duke was merely flattered by the attention. As the months went by, however, and they spent time together at the club and elsewhere, he began to respond to

(Lincoln Center Library)

Bea's affections. In late 1938 Mildred, who had heard about Bea, asked Duke if he loved the beautiful showgirl, and he answered that he thought he did. That was enough for Mildred. Early in 1939 the two were divorced, and Bea Ellis subsequently became the new Mrs. Ellington. Mildred, who eleven years before had herself been a beautiful young Cotton Club chorus girl with her whole career ahead of her, returned to Boston.

Bill Robinson and Cab Calloway shared top billing for the spring 1939 Cotton Club show, although it was clear that Robinson was the major attraction. He certainly deserved it. At age sixty he was starring simultaneously in the Cotton Club show and in Michael Todd's The Hot Mikado, staged by Hassard Short.

During the two weeks prior to the opening of the show the Cotton Club was closed, to permit all-night rehearsals. The club was in a frenzy of activity, and the performers were often exhausted and irritable. Not Bill Robinson. Shuttling back and forth between Hot Mikado and Cotton

Cab Calloway recording "Hi De Ho, Man!"
(Culver Pictures)

Club rehearsals, he put in a daily sixteen hours, first at the Broadhurst Theatre, on West Forty-fourth Street, and then at the club. At two o'clock in the morning he was bubbling with energy and humor, instructing the chorus line in the intricacies of his soft-shoe routines. A quick study, he memorized his scripts in minutes, then turned to help the others with theirs. He did not have to be so energetic at the Cotton Club rehearsals. There was no question that the Hot Mikado show took priority. In fact, out of deference to Mike Todd and the opening of Mikado, Herman Stark postponed the opening of his show four days.

It proved to be a clever decision. The Hot

Mikado was received with rave reviews. The New York Daily News gave it a XXX½ X rating, and the Telegram called it "Magnificent—loudest, craziest, hottest and most brilliantly organized jam session of this cock-eyed jazz age." It did not hurt the Cotton Club's business at all to have as the star of its show the star of a smash Broadway musical.

Relieved from the pressure of sixteen-hours-a-day rehearsals, Robinson now put in an eight-hour performing day. After the 7:30 P.M. show at the Cotton Club he dashed to the Broadhurst for the 8:40 show, then back to the Cotton Club for the midnight and 2 A.M. shows. And on Wednesdays and Saturdays there were additional afternoon matinees of The Hot Mikado.

Robinson's act at the Cotton Club did not suffer at all as a result of his Mikado performances. He was a true showman and a real professional, and the audience recognized this. Grinning from ear to ear, strutting across the floor with his shoulders thrown back, his derby tilted rakishly on his head, his feet tapping rhythmically with effortless grace, he received rave reviews at the Cotton Club as well.

Still, Cab Calloway managed to hold his own. His energetic performance, while not as awe-inspiring as that of the sixty-year-old Robinson, was a definite crowd pleaser. Leading chorus and dance numbers, swapping wisecracks with Robinson, and shouting "The Ghost of Smokey Joe," a production number in his "Minnie the Moocher" series, Calloway received his own share of mentions in the Broadway columns.

Robinson and Calloway headed a fine, talented cast. Sister Rosetta Tharpe, Stark's "find" of the previous season, lead the choir in spirituals, among which "Sunday Morning in Harlem" was considered by some the highlight of the show. She was so well received that two weeks after the

show opened, revisions were made to give her more exposure. She was allowed to leave the stage back of the orchestra pit and to come down to the floor and share the spotlight with Robinson in a special number. It brought down the house.

Other performers included dancer Tanya; Katherine Perry; Glenn and Jenkins, who with Myra Johnson did a risqué ballad; dancers Son and Sonny, whom Stark had discovered at the Grand Terrace Café in Chicago, where he had gone with Jimmie Braddock after the Louis-Braddock fight; the Beachcombers; the Six Cotton Club Boys; and Will Vodery's Choir. It was the first time that Vodery, who had been choir director and arranger at the club for a year, was given such billing.

Play: The Hot Mikado (Bill Robinson, Gwendolyn Reyde, Frances Broch, Rosetta Le Noire) (Museum of the City of New York)

Benny Davis and J. Fred Coots had left the club after writing the score for the fall 1938 show, and Ted Koehler had returned to do the songs with composer Rube Bloom. While their songs did not prove as memorable as those of some other shows, "Don't Worry 'Bout Me," "Got No Time" and "If I Were Sure of You" became respectable hits; and their "What Goes Up Must Come Down" is as familiar today as it was in 1939.

With Clarence Robinson's choreography, Frances Feist's costumes and Julian Harrison's sets, the World's Fair Edition of the Cotton Club Parade was in the best Cotton Club tradition, and it attracted record-

breaking crowds. Among those visitors during the first four nights after the show opened: J. Edgar Hoover, Clyde Tolson, night-club comedian and musical-comedy performer Eddie Garr, Mary Martin, Winthrop Rockefeller, Charlie Barnet, Hassard Short, Billy Rose, and Leo Spitz and Nate Blumber, production manager and president of Universal Pictures, respectively. During the first two weeks of the show's run the club grossed $67,000, Herman Stark reported, and an estimated 7,000 persons were turned away during the first week alone.

There was no question that the presence of the World's Fair was good for business. Visitors to the fair made it a point to visit the Cotton Club as well. To increase its attraction the club inaugurated a special series of Sunday theatrical nights, after the midnight show, to honor such stars as Jimmy Durante, Alice Faye, band leader and composer Abe Lyman, Tommy Dorsey and Sammy Kaye.

Business was so good that the Cotton Club management decided to keep the club open through the entire summer, for only the second time in its sixteen-year history. The show that played for the summer was not as ambitious as the busy-season shows, and Stark had cut down the running time of the show to one hour, although he continued his policy of presenting three shows nightly. There were few big-name acts. The comedy team of Buck and Bubbles were billed as the stars. June Richmond, Tip, Tap & Toe, Aland and Anise, Floyd Smith, Vic Terell, Tommy Wilson and Edna Mae Holley contributed their talents.

One notable addition to the roster was Andy Kirk's orchestra, which had been hired to replace Cab Calloway's band. Kirk

(Schomburg Collection, NYPL)

The Cotton Club, c. 1940. (Culver Pictures)

and his group were out of Kansas City and had been playing in New York for six years, mostly in Harlem night clubs, before being booked into the Cotton Club. While not particularly well-known to the public at large, the distinctive and original style of the Kirk band had already attracted a considerable following among record fans and members of other bands. Its guitarist, Floyd Smith, was largely responsible for the vogue of electric-guitar players in swing bands. It was his playing that had caused Benny Goodman to look for an electric guitarist back in 1938, leading to the discovery of Charlie Christian and the formation of the Goodman sextet.

The Kirk orchestra was distinctive, too, in that its one female member, a slim young girl named Mary Lou Williams, was not its vocalist but its pianist. Not only did she play the piano; she was also a composer and arranger. It was she who, having heard of the playing of swing pianist Roll 'Em Pete Johnson, composed the driving tune "Roll 'Em," which was popular with all swing bands of the day. Both this piece and her composition "Camel Walk" had been featured earlier that year in Goodman's concert with Leopold Stokowski at the Hollywood Bowl. The Kirk orchestra proved an excellent choice for the Cotton Club's summer 1939 run.

Ted Koehler and Rube Bloom were unavailable to write a score for the new summer show, so Sammy Cahn and Saul Chaplin were hired to write it. Their work for the show was not particularly memorable, but it did give Sister Rosetta Tharpe's career a boost. With the opportunity to display her talents in greater degree now that she was not billed among so awesome an array of performers, she proved a major highlight of the show. Her best song, written

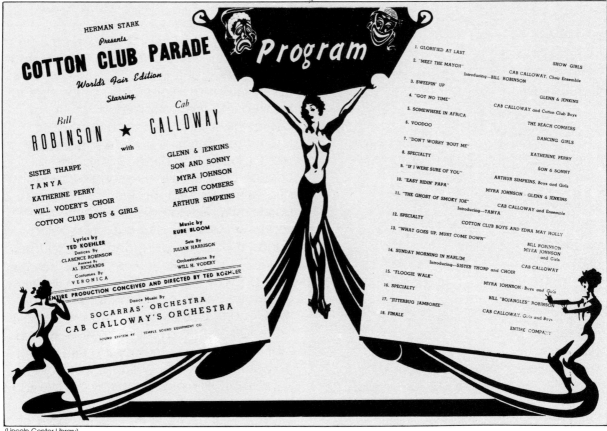

(Lincoln Center Library)

for her by Cahn and Chaplin, was "Religion on a Mule," for which she sat astride a live mule led out onto the stage. Sung as only Sister Tharpe could sing it, the song had all the spirit and rhythm of an old-fashioned Southern religious revival meeting.

The Cotton Club's summer 1939 show had hardly gotten off the ground when Herman Stark found himself wishing for a little help from above, or at least wishing he had kept his mouth shut when reporters asked him about the club's profits. On July 14, federal indictments for income-tax evasion were handed down against the Cotton Club and five other New York night clubs.

The government had launched a concerted campaign to enforce collection of taxes from night clubs and other amusement enterprises, and had decided that the most successful way to accomplish its goal was to press criminal charges, seeking prison sentences as well as fines.

The indictment naming the Cotton Club Management Corporation also accused Herman Stark, President; George Goodrich, Accountant; and Noah L. Braunstein, Secretary-Treasurer, on four counts of failure to pay, and embezzlement of taxes. Conviction could bring prison terms up to twenty years and $20,000 in fines. Other clubs indicted were Chateau Moderne, El Toreador, Man About Town Club, Little Rumanian Ron Dez Vous, and a Brooklyn club, the Royal Frolics, Jamaica.

Naturally, the Cotton Club Management

Corporation pleaded not guilty to the charges, as did the other groups and individuals indicted. But the government meant business, and eventually all paid fines. Stark had tried to head off the indictment by paying $500 on account early in the week of July 10, with a promise to pay the remainder of the $2,900 the club owed on Monday, July 17. But the indictments were handed down on Friday the 14th, leaving Stark with no choice but to go to court. Later, when the case came to trial in the fall, the Cotton Club was slapped with a hefty fine. Stark was in a bad mood that autumn.

For the first time the downtown Cotton Club was feeling the effects of the Depression. Rent at the choice Broadway site was high. So were labor costs. A club employing as many performers as the Cotton Club had a huge weekly payroll. Then, there was a stronger musicians' union with which to contend. One of its requirements was one day off per week for its members. During the summer Stark had refused to shell out the money for a fill-in crew for the one night, but once fall arrived, he had to do so. These expenses, combined with the tight federal watch on the club's accounts, which allowed for no further embezzlement or cover-up, made the club a luxury its management was fast becoming ill able to afford. An outsider would have been unable to discern the Cotton Club's money troubles. Prices did not rise, service did not decline, and the fall entertainment was as lavish as ever. In fact, the club presented two separate shows that fall.

The first show took advantage of the fact that Bill Robinson would be in town until The Hot Mikado went on tour in early November. It was a semi-vaudeville variety show, and the band hired, both for it and

the major show to follow, was Louis Armstrong's.

This was the first time Armstrong had ever played at the club, and the event was a long time in coming. He had played at just about every other major New York club featuring black entertainers, and his recordings were on juke boxes across the country. His style was not the polished Duke Ellington kind. It was not Kansas City, like Andy Kirk's, but New Orleans. Armstrong was famed for his "scat singing" of pure nonsense syllables, a style not unknown to a club that had so often featured Cab Calloway, so that was not the reason for his belated appearance at the club. Perhaps the chief reason was that the club may have considered him "a little too Negro." He was criticized in some circles for, as one columnist put it, "his ape-man antics." He was also very dark-skinned, much darker than Calloway or Ellington, and the club's policy had always been to feature Negro entertainers, but . . .

The early-fall variety show was called a "warm-up" for Armstrong. It may also have

Armstrong musicians. (Collection of Duncan Schiedt)

Opposite: Louis Armstrong.
(Museum of the City of New York)

been a trial period for Armstrong. The show was highly successful. Robinson and Armstrong were supported by the Zephyrs, Avis Andrews, Princess Orelia and Chilton & Thomas. There were no lavish sets, no high-stepping chorus lines, and Dan Healy was not even emcee; Bobby Evans filled in for him in that capacity. Still, it was a good show. As one columnist put it:

To be sure there aren't a floor full of dusky chorines doing the 1, 2, 3, nor costumes, nor big production numbers. But somehow we didn't miss them at all the other night. Girls just get in the way when the Mayor of Harlem starts strutting down the floor . . . Although such a magnificent presence just naturally needs elbow room, he does leave a little space for Louis Armstrong, whom Mr. Robinson terms the "one-man Yankee team," . . . his trumpet tooting is phenomenal.[2]

When the show closed and rehearsals began for the major show, Louis was in solid with the Cotton Club management.

And before the year was out he would be in just as solid with a beautiful chorus girl named Lucille Wilson, who back in 1932 had broken the chorus-line color bar at the Cotton Club. Louis Armstrong and Lucille Wilson got married, and their marriage lasted until Armstrong's death.

None other than the professional lazy man, Stepin Fetchit, replaced Robinson as Louis Armstrong's co-star for the big show, and if Robinson had required special arrangements at times, they were nothing compared to what Stepin Fetchit expected, and Stepin Fetchit usually got what he wanted.

He was born Lincoln Theodore Perry in Key West, Florida, son of a cigar maker. Like so many other black entertainers of the era, he started in show business early, getting into minstrel shows in 1915 at the age of thirteen. He traveled around with one show or another for ten years before reaching Hollywood in 1925, and after that he had steady work in films. Legend has it that he got his name originally from a race horse called Fetch It. The name intrigued him, and he wrote a comic song, "The Steppin' Fetch It," whose title, over the years, became his name.

O sweep of stars over
Harlem Streets,
A city dreaming to a lullaby
—Langston Hughes

Starting with small parts in such movies as In Old Kentucky (1927), The Ghost Talks (1929) and Show Boat (1929), his caricature of a lazy, no-account good-for-nothing was so successful that he became the first black actor actually to be under contract to a major studio. From 1929 to 1935 he appeared in twenty-six films, several of them with Will Rogers, often working in as many as four at a time. He made a great deal of money, and spent it lavishly. And the more Twentieth Century-Fox exploited his spending in order to promote its young black star, the more lavishly he spent. Stories circulated about his high living. He had six houses, sixteen Chinese servants, imported $2,000 cashmere suits from India, threw huge parties, and had twelve cars, one a champagne-pink Cadillac with his name in neon lights on the side. He was a star, and at the Cotton Club he expected to be treated in the style to which he was accustomed. Before arriving at the club, he informed Stark of his requirements, typing the letter himself.

Mr. Herman Starks:

This is to advise you that it will necessitate you to furnish me with a Chinese girl singer and a very light straight man for support of my original song presentation during my engagements at the Cotton Club.

Also you are to furnish the following props and costumes: a white French phone with a fifty-foot cord and a proper plug-in connection, and battery telephone bell to ring continually offstage; also, a minstrel covered chair, and tamborine; a small piano and stool; a green low-back over-stuffed parlor chair; a collapsible service tray and tea wagon; two school desks; a prop pinto horse.

Also three microphones—a long, short and table microphone, all connected for use; three school girl costumes for the Dandridge Sisters and a school teacher's outfit for principal to be selected; a minstrel outfit for me, and an interlocutor's outfit for principal to be selected; a

Opposite: Stepin Fetchit. (Lincoln Center Library)

Philip Morris uniform and maid's outfit for the Chinese girl.

Also a French artists' beret and jacket for me; and two new song arrangements each week, the music and word material I will furnish and their arrangements furnished by you; also a Will Rogers outfit and makeup for straight man.

During my engagement I can be the only one allowed to talk other than the straight man and all other acts must have fast moving routines and songs. You must furnish a new Cotton Club book to include printed matter I have in collection with these song presentations and my picture must be painted among the Cotton Club stars on the upstairs bar lobby wall in place desired by me.

Nota bene. These props, costumes, printing matter, art work and arrangements with all principals is absolutely necessary, with rehearsals at least three days before my opening. So let's get going if I am to open as we desire Wednesday night.

Regards,
Stepin Fetchit[3]

While there exists no record of Stark's response to Stepin Fetchit's letter, clearly there were some negotiations, and some compromise on Fetchit's part. When he opened at the Cotton Club he did not, for example, have "a Chinese girl singer."

The major fall show at the Cotton Club opened on November 1 at midnight. Fetchit and Armstrong presided over some fifty other performers, fewer than in most previous major shows at the club and indicating some financial belt-tightening on Stark's part. All of the lesser acts from the earlier variety show were retained and were joined, perhaps most important in the minds of many of the audience, by the Cotton Club Girls, although the line, numbering sixteen, was smaller than that of previous shows. Other additions included

Chapter 10

THE MEMORY LINGERS ON

Everything changes; nothing stays the same. It has been over a half a century since the Cotton Club opened in Harlem, and nearly that long since Harlem had its heyday. It is hard to identify the sites of the hot Harlem nightspots of the twenties today. Barron Wilkins' Exclusive Club, after going through various metamorphoses as the Theatrical Grill and the Red Pirate, is now Roy Campanella, Inc., a liquor store. The site of Connor's Café enjoyed brief success as Murray's Roseland, a Harlem version of the Broadway dance hall, in the late twenties. By the mid-sixties, the entire block had been demolished. The Nest Club became a warehouse. Of the Harlem "Big Three" of Prohibition times, only Small's Paradise remains. Now it is Big Wilt's Small's Paradise, a small bar with minor entertainment, owned by Wilt Chamberlain. The former Connie's Inn site, occupied after the Immermans moved downtown by the Ubangi Club and Birdland, is now Hilda's Admiral Café.

Opposite: Billie Holiday. (Culver Pictures)

The Harlem Cotton Club site remained vacant for a number of years after the club's downtown move. Around 1939 the downstairs section of the original Douglas Casino was converted into the Golden Gate Ballroom, where Adam Clayton Powell, Jr., held his first meeting to mobilize the people of Harlem to boycott neighborhood stores that refused to hire blacks; where, in September 1941, he announced his intention to be the first black candidate ever to run for New York's City Council; and where, on December 17, 1944, a huge gathering of Harlemites sent off to Washington, D.C., the nation's first black congressman, Adam Clayton Powell, Jr. In 1945 a new Club Sudan opened in the upstairs section of the Douglas Casino, where the Cotton Club was located. It featured Andy Kirk's orchestra. Delano Village, a middle-income private housing development, now occupies the site.

As for the Broadway Cotton Club site, two years after the Cotton Club closed, on April Fool's night, 1942, Lou Walters opened the Latin Quarter there.

The Cotton Club people, after the club closed, went their separate ways. Some remained in show business; others did not. Some were successful; others were not. Some are dead; some still live and work today. Despite their long association with organized crime, the owners and managers, Owney Madden, George "Big Frenchy" DeMange, Herman Stark, never met the fate of many mobsters. All died of natural causes and enjoyed lives of comparative respectability.

All of the Cotton Club bands were well established by the time the club closed, and Ellington and Calloway are names as familiar today as they were back in the thirties. Ellington was still accepting bookings

and had just completed his autobiography, Music Is My Mistress, when he died in 1974, leaving a legacy of some 6,000 original compositions. Cab Calloway remains active, and while his age and changing times have led to the dissolution of his "hi-de-ho" reputation, he is still one of the most energetic band leaders around. Louis Armstrong lived on to be one of the most loved entertainers in the world, universally mourned when he died in 1973. Jimmie Lunceford died tragically on July 13, 1947, much too young. Had he lived, he would undoubtedly have achieved a fame comparable to that of Ellington or Calloway or Armstrong. But although Lunceford is dead, he is by no means forgotten. His trumpeter, Sy Oliver, formed his own seven-piece group and kept the Lunceford-Oliver style alive. In July of 1975, on the occasion of the anniversary of Lunceford's death, New York's Rainbow Room featured the Oliver group in a month-long tribute to Lunceford and his celebrated band.

Ivy Anderson, who joined Ellington's band as female vocalist in 1929, remained with the band for thirteen years, until the summer of 1942. Actually, she had wanted to leave for some time. Ivy's Chicken Shack, a restaurant she had started in Los Angeles, was doing well, and she wanted to supervise the operation. After a few years, however, lonely for the stage, she returned with a solo act. She, too, died young, at the age of forty-five, in a Los Angeles apartment building managed by her husband, Robert Collins.

Harold Arlen is dead as well, but his life and career were long and successful. His list of compositions is extraordinary, but he avoided publicity to such a degree that he was always a sort of "unknown celebrity." Few who are not music buffs realize that he wrote, among other songs, "That Old Black Magic," "One for My Baby," "Let's Fall in Love," "The Man That Got Away" and

"Right as the Rain," or that he did the score for both <u>The Wizard of Oz</u>, including "Over the Rainbow," and <u>A Star Is Born</u>, Judy Garland's comeback film. It is impossible to imagine American popular music without Harold Arlen.

Only one of the Dandridge Sisters achieved stardom. "From the earliest days, members of the [Cotton Club] company told me that I should be outside the trio and on my own," Dorothy Dandridge later recalled, and eventually she became a star in films, among them <u>Porgy and Bess</u>. She is best known for her "tragic mulatto" roles, which were echoed, too dramatically, in her own life. She died in September 1965 at the age of forty-two. Her death certificate listed as the cause of death "acute drug intoxication."

After leaving the Cotton Club, Dorothy

> # If I'm elected, I'll have the Inaugural ball at the Cotton Club.
>
> —Eddie Cantor

> # For superb entertainment—always the Cotton Club.
>
> —Jascha Heifetz

> # The Cotton Club—I went for fifteen minutes and stayed three hours.
>
> —Babe Ruth

Fields, whose father had been against a career in show business for her, climbed to the top. She went on to write the lyrics for "On the Sunny Side of the Street," "Exactly Like You," "Don't Blame Me" and "I Won't Dance," as well as the words to the entire score of the Broadway musical A Tree Grows in Brooklyn. Besides Jimmy McHugh, she collaborated with Cole Porter, Jerome Kern and Harold Arlen. She and Kern won an Academy Award in 1936 for "The Way You Look Tonight," which they wrote for Swing Time. When she died, in March 1974, at the age of sixty-eight, she was up for a Tony Award for her work with composer Cy Coleman on the musical Seesaw.

Sonny Greer, Duke Ellington's famed drummer, was forced to retire from show business in the fifties due to the illness of his wife, Millicent, a former Cotton Club Girl.

Lena Horne, like Ellington, Calloway and Armstrong, needs little in the way of further identification. She became, and remains, a superstar. One of the frequent topics of discussion when her name is mentioned is her age, for she is as beautiful now as she was when she was hired at the Cotton Club in 1933. There is much speculation about her age, but if, as she said, she was "about sixteen" when she came to the Cotton Club in 1933, in 1976 she was about fifty-eight.

Bill Robinson died in November 1949, but his memory lives on. While he left no songs like an Ellington or an Arlen, he left a presence that is still felt today and is expressed in the song "Mr. Bojangles."

Clarence Robinson, manager of the Standard Theatre in Philadelphia when Duke Ellington was playing there and the Cotton Club wanted him, and later choreographer and director at the club itself, is still active. In July 1975, he was at the Kennedy Center in Washington, D.C.

Ethel Waters has become a legend. The fat, good-natured, dignified and all-knowing strong-black-woman characters she later played are so ingrained in the American mind that it is hard for many to imagine that she once sang adult "torch songs" in Harlem dives. She became as beloved, in her field, as Louis Armstrong did in his.

Elida Webb, choreographer at the Cotton Club until 1934 served as choreographer for Running Wild. She married Garfield Dawson, known as "The Strutter" and an active dancer until his retirement in 1973 when he was eighty-one. Two years later, on May 1, 1975, Elida Webb Dawson died at the age of seventy-nine.

Being individuals first and entertainers second, before and sometimes after being

Nostalgia has not played anyone false about the Cotton Club shows. They were wonderful.

—Lena Horne

Former Cotton Club entertainers recall some glorious moments at their reunion in 1960.
(Johnson Publishing Co.)

at the Cotton Club, most remember it with bitterness or fondness. But they do not dwell on it. Those who were part of the group then associated forever after the club with the group. For the Cotton Club Boys and Girls, the Cotton Club was like a school, and after the club closed they regrouped periodically, like the alumni classes of a high school or college.

After the Cotton Club closed, the Cotton Club Boys remained together for about a year. They toured with Cab Calloway for six months, then together as an independent unit, giving their last show at the Hippodrome in Baltimore. Fourteen years after the closing of the Cotton Club, the Boys, who started at $45 a week and were making $125 six years later when the club closed, held a reunion at the Club Sudan. Intending to comprise all the Cotton Club Boys, from the time the group was formed until the Broadway club closed, they were shy four members. Roy Carter had died in 1934, just a few months after the group was formed. Al Alstock died of tuberculosis in 1937. Ernest Frazier also died of tuberculosis, in 1949, and in 1950 Walter Shepherd died.

Of the Cotton Club Boys who reunited in 1954, only one had remained in show business steadily. Charlie Atkins went on to teach at the Katherine Dunham School and to dance professionally with Honey Coles, who in 1975 was with Harlem's famed Apollo Theatre. Jimmy Wright and Tommy Porter did occasional television and radio roles for a while, but the former Cotton Club Boys seemed to have become primarily bartenders and salesmen. Jules Adger, considered the lady-killer of the line, went to law school, completing his

studies at St. John's University in 1955. Maxie Armstrong, after sporadic postwar night-club work, became a clerk with the U.S. Postal Service. William Smith, at the time of the reunion, was a swimming instructor at the Harlem YMCA. Eddie Morton became a bartender and moved to Detroit. Roy "Chink" Porter, who replaced Tommy Porter in the line in 1937, owned and operated a bar in Harlem. Freddie Heron worked at Harlem's Silver Rail Bar, and Warren Coleman also operated his own bar in Harlem.

The Cotton Club Girls also had reunions, although those who attended them were primarily the ones who had, voluntarily or involuntarily, left show business when the Cotton Club closed. One exception was the former Edna Mae Holly, who married Sugar Ray Robinson, and who rarely failed to·attend one of the many reunions. Altogether, some 150 girls worked in the Cotton Club chorus line. Some married stars or important men: Isabel Washington, who

became the first Mrs. Adam Clayton Powell, Jr.; Edna Mae Holly; Lucille Wilson, who married Louis Armstrong; and Peggy Griffiths, whose light skin color aroused much controversy over her racial identity and who married a wealthy New Jersey lawyer.

Others continued to work, but rarely in show business. Tondelayo, who started in the line and later became an exotic-dancer specialty act, opened Tondelayo's Melody Room in Harlem, employing Margaret Cheraux, another former Cotton Club Girl, as a cashier. Mildred Dixon, who was divorced from Duke Ellington in 1939, went to work in 1945 as office manager for a sheet-music publishing firm. Hyacinth Curtis worked for a while at the Club Zanzibar after the Cotton Club closed, and then toured with the USO before becoming a dental technician. Evelyn Sheppard married a Harlem bar owner, Jack Fuller. Carolyn Rich Henderson became a salesgirl in a Fifth Avenue shop. Ethel Sissle divorced band leader Noble Sissle and married an

> The universe is a spiraling Big Band in a polka-dotted speakeasy, effusively generating new light every one-night stand.
>
> —Ishmael Reed

attorney in Los Angeles named Walter Gordon, Jr. Maudine Simmons married Chicago Brass Rail owner Nelson Sykes.

In October 1948, several of the girls who had maintained close contact with each other since the club folded, decided to start an association of all the girls who had ever worked in the Cotton Club chorus or as showgirls. Response to the idea was very favorable, and the group that was formed was named the Cotton Club Girls Association, Inc. The officers: Hyacinth Curtis, president; Juanita Boisseau, vice-president; Carolyn Rich Henderson, secretary; Billye Schwab, treasurer; and Vivian Jackson, chargé d'affaires. They held reunions, to which males who had been associated with the Cotton Club were of course invited, and maintained a newsletter to inform members of each other's activities.

Such associations helped keep memories vivid for those who were associated with the club. But over the years the Cotton Club has been kept alive in the minds of the general public through a series of "revivals" of the famous Cotton Club shows. Called Cotton Club Revues, they have often featured the talents who worked at the Cotton Club. Cab Calloway has initiated and starred in a number of them; Clarence Robinson has directed and/or choreographed several; and Benny Davis, minus J. Fred Coots, has staged and developed some. In 1976 Bubbling Brown Sugar, a musical recalling the Cotton Club era and seeming to have taken its name from the club's 1930 show, Brown Sugar—Sweet, But Unrefined, opened on Broadway, featuring dancer Avon Long. Cotton Club Revues have also provided showcases for young talents who never knew the Cotton Club. Comedian George Kirby, dancer Lonnie Satin and singer Denise Rogers have, over the years, received needed exposure, and in 1957 a young singer named Abbey Lincoln sang "The Battle of Jericho" in a Revue that headlined Cab Calloway. Some older talents who never saw the inside of the Cotton Club have also benefited from the drive to keep the club alive in America's mind. Redd Foxx headlined one of the Revues in 1961 and was praised in Variety for his clever and rapid delivery, although it was pointed out that he too often crossed the "pornographic border."

The Revues have tried to recapture the mood, the feeling, of the Old Cotton Club, and many of the featured tunes are those that were made famous at the club. In a sense, it is difficult to understand their attraction and success, for the Cotton Club is of another time, of an era in which an entirely different mood prevailed. But places frequented by "the beautiful people" never lose their attraction, and there are few similar spots in American history that have produced the formidable array of talent and creative material that came out of the Cotton Club.

Bibliography

BOOKS

Arstein, Helen, and Moss, Carlton, eds., In Person—Lena Horne. New York: Greenburg, 1950.

Bogle, Donald, Toms, Coons, Mulattoes, Mammies & Bucks. New York: Viking, 1973.

Chartres, Samuel B., and Kunstadt, Leonard, Jazz: A History of the New York Scene. Garden City, N.Y.: Doubleday, 1962.

Collier, James Lincoln, Inside Jazz. New York: Four Winds Press, 1973.

Dance, Stanley, The World of Duke Ellington. New York: Scribner's, 1970.

Dandridge, Dorothy, and Conrad, Earl, Everything and Nothing: The Dorothy Dandridge Tragedy. New York: Abelard-Schuman, 1970.

De Leeuw, Hendrik, Sinful Cities of the Western World. New York: Citadel Press, 1934.

Durante, Jimmy, and Kofoed, Jack, Night Clubs. New York: Knopf, 1931.

Ellington, Duke, Music Is My Mistress. Garden City, N.Y.: Doubleday, 1973.

Horne, Lena, and Schickel, Richard, Lena. Garden City, N.Y.: Doubleday, 1965.

Huggins, Nathan, Harlem Renaissance. New York: Oxford University Press, 1971.

Hughes, Langston, The Big Sea. New York: Knopf, 1940.

————, Famous Negro Music Makers. New York: Dodd, Mead, 1955.

————, and Meltzer, Milton, Black Magic: A Pictorial History of the Negro in American Entertainment. Englewood Cliffs, N.J.: Prentice-Hall, 1967.

Jablonski, Edward, Harold Arlen: Happy with the Blues. Garden City, N.Y.: Doubleday, 1961.

Johnson, James Weldon, Black Manhattan. New York: Atheneum paperback edition, 1968.

Kellner, Bruce, Carl Van Vechten and the Irreverent Decades. Norman, Okla.: University of Oklahoma Press, 1968.

Kimball, Robert, and Bolcum, William, Reminiscing with Sissle and Blake. New York: Viking, 1973.

Lambert, G. E., Duke Ellington. New York: Barnes, 1961.

Locke, Alain, and Stern, Bernhard, eds., When Peoples Meet: A Study of Race and Culture Contrasts. New York: Progressive Educational Association, 1942.

Loos, Anita, A Girl Like I. New York: Viking, 1966.

McKay, Claude, Harlem: Negro Metropolis. New York: Dutton, 1940.

————, Home to Harlem. New York: Harper, 1928.

Mezzrow, Mezz, and Wolfe, Bernard, Really the Blues. New York: Random House, 1946.

Osofsky, Gilbert, Harlem: The Making of a Ghetto. New York: Harper, 1963.

Ottley, Roi, and Weatherby, William S., eds. The Negro in New York: An Informal Social History. New York: The New York Public Library, Oceana Publications, 1967.

Powell, Adam Clayton, Adam by Adam. New York: Dial, 1971.

Shapiro, Nat, and Hentoff, Nat, Hear Me Talkin to Ya. New York: Dover, 1955.

Shaw, Charles G., Night Life: Vanity Fair's Intimate Guide to New York After Dark. New York: John Day, 1931.

Sillman, Leonard, Here Lies Leonard Sillman. New York: Citadel, 1959.

Sobol, Louis, The Longest Street. New York: Crown, 1968.

Sylvester, Robert, No Cover Charge: A Backward Look at the Night Clubs. New York: Dial, 1956.

Ulanov, Barry, Duke Ellington. New York: Creative Age, 1946.

Van Vechten, Carl, Nigger Heaven. New York: Harper, Colophon edition, 1971.

Walker, Danton, Danton Walker's Guide to New York Night Life. New York: Putnam's, 1958.

Waters, Ethel, and Samuels, Charles, His Eye Is
    on the Sparrow. Garden City, N.Y.: Double-
    day, 1951.
Williams, Martin T., The Art of Jazz. New York:
    Oxford University Press, 1959.

Morris, George Chester, "Harlem Revisited."
    Commonweal (March 3, 1935),
    11–12.
"Operas and Cabarets." The Messenger, Vol. 6,
    No. 3 (March 1924), 71.

ARTICLES

"Cotton Club Girls." Ebony (April 1949), 34–38.
Cromwell, Chester T., "The World's Largest
    Negro City." Saturday Evening Post, Vol.
    198 (August 8, 1925), 8–9.
Edmonds, Randolph, "Not Many of Your People
    Come Here." The Messenger, Vol. 10, No. 3
    (March 1928), 57+.
Fisher, Rudolph, "The Caucasian Storms Har-
    lem." American Mercury, Vol. 11 (August
    1927), 393–98.
Kennedy, John B., "So This Is Harlem!" Collier's
    (October 28, 1933), 22+.
Lane, Winthrop D., "Ambushed in the City: The
    Grim Side of Harlem." Survey, Vol. 53
    (March 1, 1925), 692–94+.

EPHEMERA

Museum of the City of New York, Theater and
    Music Collection; Photo Library
New York Daily News, various years
New York Post, various years
New York Public Library, Astor, Lenox and Tilden
    Foundations, Lincoln Center for the Perform-
    ing Arts Library, vertical files, Lester Sweyd
    Collection
New York Public Library, Astor, Lenox and Tilden
    Foundations, Schomburg Center for
    Research in Black Culture, vertical files, Fed-
    eral Writers Project: Negroes in New York;
    Picture Collection
New York Times, various years
Variety, various years

Notes

CHAPTER 1

1 Randolph Edmonds, "Not Many of Your People Come Here," the Messenger.

2 Liner Notes, "The Sound of Harlem," Jazz Odyssey, Vol. III, Columbia Archive Series.

3 "Operas and Cabarets," the Messenger.

4 Leonard Sillman, Here Lies Leonard Sillman, p. 96.

5 Langston Hughes, The Big Sea, p. 225.

6 Alain Locke and Bernard Stern, eds. When Peoples Meet: A Study in Race and Culture Contrasts, p. 345.

7 Rudolph Fisher, "The Caucasian Storms Harlem," American Mercury.

8 Edmonds, p. 57.

9 Hendrik De Leeuw, Sinful Cities of the Western World, pp. 261–63.

CHAPTER 2

1 Jimmy Durante and Jack Kofoed, Night Clubs, p. 114.

2 Ibid, p. 115.

3 Edward Jablonski, Harold Arlen: Happy with the Blues, p. 35.

CHAPTER 3

1 Duke Ellington, Music Is My Mistress, pp. 75–76.

2 Douglas Watt, "Some Friendly Hoods; Met on a Ballet Kick," New York Daily News (March 17, 1959).

3 Emory Lewis, "Her Words Are Legend," Jersey Record (May 27, 1973).

4 Stanley Dance, The World of Duke Ellington, p. 67.

5 Barry Ulanov, Duke Ellington, p. 114.

6 Robert Sylvester, No Cover Charge: A Backward Look at the Night Clubs, p. 55.

7 Ibid, p. 51.

8 Ibid, p. 50.

9 Ibid, p. 45.

CHAPTER 4

1 Mezz Mezzrow and Bernard Wolfe, Really the Blues, p. 212.

2 Interview with Cab Calloway.

3 "The Carnation Kid," Downbeat (January 15, 1947).

4 Newspaper clipping, no date, Lincoln Center for the Performing Arts Library.

5 Adam Clayton Powell, Jr., Adam by Adam, p. 222.

6 Sylvester, No Cover Charge, p. 63.

7 Jablonski, Harold Arlen, p. 68.

CHAPTER 5

1 Ethel Waters with Charles Samuels, His Eye Is on the Sparrow, p. 219.

2 Ibid, p. 220.

3 Jablonski, Harold Arlen, p. 76.

4 Lena Horne and Richard Schickel, Lena, pp. 47–48.

5 Ibid., pp. 48–49.

CHAPTER 6

1 Louis Sobol, The Longest Street, p. 54.

2 Helen Arstein and Carlton Moss, eds., In Person—Lena Horne. pp. 50–51.

3 Ibid, pp. 46–47.

4 Adam Clayton Powell, Jr., "Sharecroppers," Amsterdam News (November 17, 1936).

5 Hughes, The Big Sea, p. 335.

CHAPTER 7

1 Sobol, The Longest Street, p. 81.

2 Newspaper clipping, no date, Lincoln Center for the Performing Arts Library.

3 Ulanov, Duke Ellington, pp. 188–89.

thing and Nothing: The Dorothy Dandridge Tragedy, p. 44.

5 Ibid., p. 45.

6 Ibid., p. 43.

7 Ibid., p. 46.

8 Ibid., pp. 42–43.

CHAPTER 8

1 Newspaper clipping, no date, Lincoln Center for the Performing Arts Library.

2 Newspaper clippng, no date, Lincoln Center for the Performing Arts Library.

3 Ibid.

4 Dorothy Dandridge and Earl Conrad, Every-

CHAPTER 9

1 Ulanov, Duke Ellington, p. 207.

2. Newspaper clipping, no date, Lincoln Center for the Performing Arts Library.

3 Newspaper clipping, no date, Lincoln Center for the Performing Arts Library.

Index

About the Author

Jim Haskins has published some thirty books
for general and juvenile audiences, as well as numerous magazine
articles. Also a free-lance educational consultant,
he lives on Manhattan's Upper West Side.